Beaufighters in the Night

Beaufighters in the Night

The 417th Night Fighter Squadron USAAF

Braxton 'Brick' Eisel

Pen & Sword
AVIATION

First published in Great Britain in 2007 by
Pen & Sword Aviation
an imprint of
Pen & Sword Books Ltd
47 Church Street
Barnsley
South Yorkshire
S70 2AS

ISBN 978 1 84415 483 8

A CIP catalogue record for this book is
available from the British Library

Typeset in 11/13 Sabon by
Lamorna Publishing Services

Printed and bound in England by Biddles Ltd.

Pen & Sword Books Ltd. incorporates the imprints of Pen & Sword Aviation,
Pen & Sword Maritime, Pen & Sword Military, Wharncliffe Local History,
Pen & Sword Select, Pen & Sword Military Classics and Leo Cooper.

For a complete list of Pen & Sword titles please contact
PEN & SWORD BOOKS LIMITED
47 Church Street, Barnsley, South Yorkshire, S70 2AS, England
E-mail: enquiries@pen-and-sword.co.uk
Website: www.pen-and-sword.co.uk

Contents

Acknowledgements

I am grateful to the men and their families of the 417th Night Fighter Squadron, particularly those that served as wartime historians and peacetime squadron representatives. Due to their efforts and diligence for the past sixty plus years, the treasure trove of material they gathered made writing this book far easier than otherwise might be the case. Although I used much of that material along with interviews and correspondence with surviving squadron members or their families, any mistakes in this work are entirely my own.

I would like to thank Walter Boyne for his unstinting help and encouragement for this project and for taking on a rookie writer. I would also like to thank a former boss and current friend, Dr Bill Head, for hiring an old crewdog as part of his Warner Robins Air Logistics Center History Office a while back.

I am honoured to have served my country and while doing so, worked with some of the finest, most talented men and women one could ever hope to meet.

To my children, Patrick, Casey and Emily, thanks for giving me the time to write. Finally, to my wife, Linda, herself a serving US Air Force officer (obviously she outranks me at home, but in uniform as well!), I thank you for your support, energy and love of life.

Introduction

They were seventeen, eighteen, nineteen, maybe twenty or twenty-one years old. They came mostly from America's farms and small towns, but back then America was mostly farms and small towns. They played a unique, unheralded role in aerial warfare. They may have shortened the war. They did help save the world. This is their story.

CHAPTER 1

What a rotten night for flying. Colder than death, a steady 20-knot wind, occasionally gusting to 40 or more, sliced right through your clothes no matter how many layers you piled on. Frequent snow and rain squalls scudded through to add to the misery.

Nevertheless, throughout the night of 27/28 December 1944, at the height of the Battle of the Bulge, nothing halted the regular flow of aeroplanes launched into the bleak sky to look for wily, elusive and dangerous enemy craft.

One of those aircraft flew into history that night. First Lieutenant Malcolm 'Duff' Campbell, pilot, and radar operator Second Lieutenant Robert 'Bob' McCullen crewed the night fighter, callsign WASTENOT 81.

They were part of the 417th Night Fighter Squadron. Since September 1944, it had been based at the windy, dirt strip at Le Vallon, not far from Marseilles in southern France. The squadron's 'beat' or patrol area included the important harbour of Marseilles, the northern part of the Mediterranean Sea, and inland to central France.

The *Luftwaffe* made numerous forays against the crowded harbour and massed shipping there, including night attacks. The 417th was placed there to foil those attacks.

For several months they did just that, fighting several engagements, but mainly by providing a deterrent to the *Luftwaffe* with their presence.

Then in early December 1944, the squadron commander and intelligence officer received several visitors from the 12th Air Force intelligence office. The 12th Air Force had specific operational control of the 417th and several other night fighter squadrons. This was an unusual command relationship in that normally a tactical squadron reported to a group headquarters, which in turn worked for a wing. The wing then reported to an Army Air Force. The 12th's commander felt that the few night fighter units were best utilized under his direct control.

These intelligence officers brought specific information about a Nazi operation to take gold, cash and some of the looted treasure of Europe, as well as Nazi Party figures themselves from an airfield in northern Italy to Barcelona, Spain.

Spain being both neutral in the war and sympathetic to the Nazi regime was a natural hideout for those Germans prescient enough to know the war was not going well. The valuables made a ready-made source of income to keep them in style once the war ended.

The Allies, all the way up to the Supreme Commander, General Dwight Eisenhower, thought, however, that the money and refugee-run might be a gambit to keep the Nazi regime alive in Spain and thus keep the war going. Intelligence had enough evidence about the existence of these flights to give them a nickname, 'Barcelona Charlie'. Eisenhower wanted these flights intercepted and stopped.

The men from 12th Air Force passed on those orders to the 417th. So, in addition to its standing duties of ship convoy escort, coastal patrol, armed reconnaissance, as well as its primary duty of night fighting, the 417th sent aloft extra patrols to intercept and destroy Barcelona Charlie. Beginning on 12 December, they launched sortie after sortie to catch him. However, it turned out to be much harder than was first imagined.

American and British ground-controlled intercept (GCI) radar stations strung along the French coastline detected only faint traces of an unknown blip along the route that Charlie was supposed to be taking. Moreover, it was at extremely low level, right on the deck.

On the few occasions when the GCI sites had something more substantial to track, they vectored a 417th plane onto the target. The primitive first-generation radars of the night fighters could not see through the clutter sent back to their scopes due to the target being lost amidst the energy reflected back by the Mediterranean. On the even rarer occasions when the airborne fighter did detect a plane, the crew had to descend to dangerously low levels to try and identify the target. At night and just above the waves no one could see the elusive aircraft – but he was there. The night fighter crews began to feel that it would take a submarine to get under him and shoot him down!

At last, on 28 December, Campbell and McCullen discovered Charlie, in unbelievably bad weather in almost impossible flying conditions. The crew's mount, like all those of the 417th, was the British-made Bristol Beaufighter. A big, twin-engined tail-dragger, the 'Beau' had served as the first effective British night fighter back in 1940 and soldiered on still, although most of the RAF night fighter squadrons had traded in theirs for night variants of the de Havilland Mosquito.

The Beau was quite a change from the Douglas P-70 that the Americans had trained on. Its big 1,670 hp Hercules sleeve-valved radial engines sat even with the cockpit, which was perched on the nose, while the rest of the aircraft trailed aft, making it a challenge to handle.

A former 417th pilot, Dr Morris 'Dirty' Dalton said:

A lot of guys complained about the Beau, but I enjoyed flying it. You had to fly it every minute, and the tail would swing on you in a heartbeat if you let it, but if you paid attention, it did what you wanted.

On take-off, you wanted to get the tail up fast so the rudder was effective. You could use differential throttles to keep straight but that was usually more work than it was worth, just pour the coals to it and get the tail up and you'd be OK.

Likewise, on landing, you kept flying it all the way to the ground. If you got slow, it would drop like a brick. After you landed, however, the pneumatic brakes on it weren't much good. Since our aircraft were borrowed from the Brits anyway, they usually gave us 'clapped out' planes with worn-out brakes. Combine that with a supply system that didn't work since we couldn't get parts for the Beau and, well, you had an 'iffy' airplane.

[The US only used four squadrons of Beaufighters, the 414th –

417th.]

When scheduled for a mission, Dalton says the mission was usually preceded by a night flying test to make sure the aircraft and its many systems were working before they left on patrol.

> We would take a Beau up for thirty minutes or so and check out the aircraft, fire up the radar to make sure it was giving a good picture and so on. I usually didn't test fire the four 20mm cannons because if I did, then the armourers would have to clean the guns after I got back. A lot of other guys did test fires on a bunch of old landing barges down off the coast, but I rarely did. I trusted the ground guys to do their job and I didn't want to make extra work for them if I didn't have to.

As for flying the Beau on patrol, he says:

> The Beau had great visibility. I had a big flat panel in front of me and large side windows. Being way up front, I could see in every direction except directly behind me and my R/O [radar operator, located in a bubble top seat near the tail] would keep an eye out there.
>
> With no superchargers, it wouldn't get very high. I can remember trying to intercept a German photo ship that would fly over Marseilles every few nights. He would be in the twenties [20,000 plus], and I'd be hanging on the props at maybe nineteen. Never could get a shot at him.
>
> At lower altitudes, I thought it handled well. It had pretty good manoeuvrability and wasn't really heavy on the controls.

Dalton recalls his experiences in chasing Barcelona Charlie:

> Our squadron got detailed to stop this run so we patrolled for weeks in December, in some of the worst weather you can imagine. The Germans had a radar altimeter coupled to an autopilot and would routinely fly at 20-30 ft above the water.
>
> Whenever we got a crack at him, which wasn't often because it was difficult to see him on radar that low, our guys had their hands full. We didn't have an autopilot so we were trying to intercept this guy, at night, in bad weather, right on the waves.

I usually set my radar altimeter to 50 ft so that if I got too close, I'd get a big old red light to get my attention. I never had a crack at him, but one of our crews finally did on the night of 28 December 1944.

Taking off at 1740 local time, Campbell and McCullen climbed their Beaufighter into the already dark French winter sky. Taking up a patrol line south-east of Marseilles, the crew began its ritual of test firing the aircraft weapons and warming up the sometimes baulky radar equipment. Unfortunately, the radar was usually the only thing that could be warmed up. The Beaufighter was notorious for being an icebox to fly. The heater was simply incapable of fighting off the cold, particularly at altitude.

At 2118, the GCI station Flametree radioed a low-altitude contact for the crew to investigate. Due to the very real possibility of the intercepted aircraft being friendly, all intercepts had to go to visual range before the crew could fire. Thus, WASTENOT 81 snapped to a heading of 160 degrees and began a steep descent. Flametree continued providing vectors until the unknown aircraft travelled into the GCI site Galley's radar coverage area. Galley continued providing target updates and positioning the approaching fighter for the 'merge'.

McCullen saw the blip on his scope at a range of 1,000 ft and took over the intercept. Realizing the target was very low, he continued refining the geometry of the intercept, attempting to place his pilot in the most tactically advantageous position directly behind and slightly below the target. This tactic provided a good position both to identify a target and, in the event it was a 'bandit', to open fire at the best offensive position for the fighter.

Down, down, down until the radar altimeter of the Beau read only 20 ft, the crew closed the range on the target. At 2130, Campbell saw it slightly to his left at a distance of 600 ft. Campbell identified the target aircraft as a Junkers Ju 290, a large four-engined long range *Luftwaffe* transport/reconnaissance aircraft. McCullen, looking up from his scope through the clear Plexiglas bubble over his seat, confirmed the identification.

Never very numerous, with fewer than seventy produced, the Ju 290 was a huge aircraft for its day. As part of KG 200, the

Luftwaffe's special-operations wing, it had a proven history of unorthodox long-range missions to its credit. Skimming the water's surface at less than 100 ft, at night, took a lot of courage on the part of the crew. The Beaufighter, coming in *below* the Ju 290, was also loaded with guts at this point.

The German aircraft was thundering along at 240 knots, on a heading of 270 degrees when Campbell pressed the firing button on the Beau's yoke. The five-second burst scored hits on the starboard inner engine of the target. With that engine afire, the big bird began what was described in the crew's combat report as 'moderate' evasive manoeuvres to try and escape. 'Moderate' at less than 100 ft above the sea had to be a white-knuckle experience for both the Axis and the Allied airmen.

Campbell hung on to the twisting target, with McCullen continuing to maintain radar contact just in case. A second run produced more damage but the enemy pressed on. Campbell closed again for a third time from the starboard side. This final burst from 500 ft sent the big plane plunging into the Mediterranean some 80 miles south-east of the Hyeras Islands, off the coast of southern France.

Campbell immediately climbed away from his position scant feet above the still-hungry waves, and back to a more sensible altitude. The crew, shaking off the combined effects of adrenalin and triumph, reported a 'grand slam' in the military radio vernacular of the times to Galley and started what must have been a very satisfying trip back to base. The next day, air-sea rescue aircraft searched the crash site and reported only what looked like planks, possibly from crates, remaining on the surface of the Mediterranean.

For their efforts, both Campbell and McCullen won Distinguished Flying Crosses (DFCs). Additionally, the 417th was honoured with a Distinguished Unit Citation in June 1945 for its efforts involved in bringing down this elusive threat.

Lieutenant Campbell died ten days after VE Day, on 18 May 1945, while flying a captured Messerschmitt Bf-109 near Pilsen, Czechoslovakia. Wing headquarters directed that those captured aircraft that were salvageable be put into flying shape and brought back to the home airfield. The 417th's mechanics with assistance from *Luftwaffe* technicians who were now prisoners of war, put the 109 back into shape.

With a high-performance engine, stubby wings, and a very narrow landing gear, the Bf-109 was a tricky aeroplane to fly, even for the experienced German pilots that trained on it. For an American to just jump in and take off took courage. Campbell was the only one to volunteer to fly it.

Unfortunately, he was not up to the challenge. He did get it started, taxied to the runway and roared aloft. Soon after getting airborne, however, the massive torque from the propeller snap rolled the aircraft to the left. Campbell was not able to recover at such a low altitude and the former German fighter claimed another victim by slamming into the ground. The aircraft burst into flames on impact and Campbell perished in the fire.

Lieutenant McCullen survived the war and returned to civilian life in New Jersey. In 1950, he was recalled to active duty due to the Korean War and resumed his role as an electronic warrior. He died in an off-duty accident in 1960, having achieved the rank of Major.

CHAPTER 2

America entered World War II unprepared for battle in many areas. One of which was night aerial combat. Indeed, until just a few years earlier, the thought of trying to shoot down an aircraft using another aircraft was considered ludicrous.

During World War I, a few of the notorious German Zeppelins had been downed by Royal Flying Corps fighters at night, but only because of a bright moon or searchlight illumination of the giant gasbag. Of course, it required a giant measure of courage for the young men to go aloft to hunt the dreaded Zeppelins, as well as the German Gotha bombers, but the number of squadrons devoted to the night defence of Great Britain did not justify the results. The science of night fighting had not really advanced much since that time.

Then in the mid-1930s, the British again turned their thoughts to what would happen if the blatantly militant Nazi Germany mounted a night bombing offensive against them. The Royal Air Force (RAF), in conjunction with some of the keenest scientific minds in the British universities and industrial institutions developed radar into a practical tool for detecting aircraft.

The story of radar in turning the tide during the Battle of Britain has been told often, but suffice it to say that America was well behind her UK cousins in this area. Indeed, the US military in the form of the US Army's Signal Corps, only conducted its first official tests with radar in 1937. The equipment was large, heavy and very bulky. Using it on board an aircraft was only a fanciful dream then.

Using ground-based radar stations spread along the eastern and southern coasts of Britain, the RAF raised an electronic shield that could detect aircraft up to 150 miles away or more, depending on their altitude. The information thus provided was passed to fighter directors who 'scrambled' or launched day fighter squadrons as needed to attack incoming *Luftwaffe* bombing raids.

Eventually, these daytime attacks became too costly for the Germans and they turned to the night to provide cover for their lumbering, vulnerable bombers. If the RAF fighters could not see them, then the *Luftwaffe* could not be shot down.

The British, however, continued to refine radar technology until by 1939 they had several hand-made radar sets installed aboard a few twin-engined aircraft. During the early days of this equipment, reliability and 'user-friendliness' left much to be desired. They learned many hard, painful lessons during the Blitz, the nearly four-month straight pounding the *Luftwaffe* delivered against London and other English cities during the winter of 1940.

Continuing their use of radar and tactics to defeat an airborne aggressor, the RAF developed GCI stations. At these small outposts, a team of technicians, men and women, operated smaller radars, a set of very high frequency (VHF) radios and the necessary power-generating equipment. An officer controller sat at a radar screen with the 'blip' of an unknown aircraft coming into the area. He then called up a night-fighter aircraft that was probably flying up and down a designated patrol line waiting for just such a call.

The controller then directed the night fighter to an interception until its own on-board radar system could detect the other aeroplane. At this point, the night-fighter crew took control of the intercept, positioning their aircraft in the best tactical position first to identify the unknown aircraft and then to shoot it down if it was an enemy. The effective range of the airborne radar was usually only 1 – 3 miles, so the controller had to be precise in his directions to the crew to make the intercept.

Once the night fighter did obtain contact (and this was never a certainty), the radar operator in the plane gave directions or 'vectors' to his pilot until the latter could get a 'visual' on the other aircraft. At that point, the pilot took over the intercept, flying his aircraft into the best position, usually astern and slightly below the enemy. Finally came the moment of truth. The pilot put the pipper of his gunsight on the target, now positively identified and pressed the trigger button.

If all went as planned, the bandit started burning and blew up shortly thereafter. Many times it did not go as planned and the now-alerted enemy began wildly manoeuvring to avoid being shot down. The night-fighter crew did their best to stay in the fight, but that was not always possible. The bandit might escape into the thick cloud cover of England, the night fighter might run out of ammunition or suffer from mechanical failures or be struck by return fire, or a myriad of other things could turn a nice, quiet case of murder into an inconclusive duel in the dark.

Under pressure to stop the *Luftwaffe*'s morale-sapping night attacks, the RAF also tried a number of other night defences. One of these was a variation of the still developing night-fighter force. Instead of putting the radar and observer in the armed aircraft, the Turbinlite operations equipped a twin-engined Douglas Boston light bomber with a very powerful searchlight in the nose instead of guns or cannons. The 'shooter' would be a Hawker Hurricane flying close formation on the Boston. The theory was that the Turbinlite Boston would detect a bandit through GCI and its own on-board radar and close on the unsuspecting enemy. When it was in close, the Boston would illuminate the intruder and the Hurricane would close in and blaze away at it.

Theory and reality were two different things. Besides the headaches of flying night formation in a single-seat day fighter like the Hurricane with the radar-equipped Boston over a blacked-out countryside in usually abysmal weather, the fighter usually lost contact with the Boston on the occasions where an enemy was brought to combat and then had to be responsible for navigating his way home and landing in the dark with no aids besides, maybe, dimly glowing paraffin lamps.

The plan also did not allow for the actions of the German aircraft if it suddenly found itself lit up by a searchlight. The enemy pilot would do everything he could to get out of the beam and back into the relative comfort of the night. In close, the Boston could not hang onto any contact like that and what is more, its powerful light made a wonderful beacon for any prowling intruder interested in scoring his own kill.

Obviously, this cumbersome system did not work well, with only one confirmed kill being recorded and numerous Hurricanes being lost due to accidents. The RAF discontinued Turbinlite operations in early 1943.

From those painful lessons, paid for in blood, the RAF developed an effective night-fighter force. Once America entered the fray, the RAF gladly agreed to help them in this arcane art. America, mainly in the form of the United States Army Air Forces (USAAF, also referred to as the 'Army Air Force') reluctantly accepted this help. Rather like the younger brother taking advice and help from an elder, the USAAF learned from the British and then tried to 'one-up' them in night fighting as well as many other areas.

The USAAF leadership, under Major General Henry 'Hap' Arnold, sent some of their most trusted subordinates to England during that country's trials of the Battle of Britain and the Blitz. From those observers, the USAAF learned many lessons, one of which was the need for an effective night-fighter force. Colonel Ira Eaker, later commanding general of the US Eighth Air Force, was one of those observers. He reported back:

> They [the RAF] believe that there should be a specialized night fighter, probably a 2-engine plane, of sufficient speed to overhaul the fast night-bomber, probably with a 50-mile differential in favor of the fighter. They should have armor forward, but there would be no requirement for armor in the rear. They should have sufficient armament of heavy caliber to knock down the heavy bomber and pierce the heaviest armor. They must have sufficient ceiling to reach all bombers .... . They thought the Beaufighter, now in use as a night fighter, had many desirable characteristics but that a plane of this type should have good stability, greater ease of control in instrument flying and a higher speed. They pointed out also to the advisability of having a plane of good landing characteristics on account of the many times when a night fighter has to land in poor visibility. The vision forward in a night fighter is a big feature since the pilot relies on outside vision generally under conditions of darkness and poor visibility for the location of his target after minimum AI [airborne interception

radar] range is reached.

Arnold turned to the quickly burgeoning US aviation industry to turn out a US-made night fighting plane. Northrop Aviation submitted the winning design, the amazing P-61 'Black Widow'.

A very big, twin-engined, twin-boomed three-man fighter, the P-61 was a revolution in aircraft design and technology. Unfortunately, all that new technology development took time America no longer had. In fact, the P-61, first ordered in January 1941, did not fly as a prototype until May 1942, and operational models did not appear until October 1943. In the meantime, US airmen needed something that could take to the night skies immediately.

The first attempt was the Douglas P-70, a modified A-20 Havoc twin-engined ground-attack bomber. The A-20 was also known as the Boston in RAF service. It was a very capable ground-attack plane, rugged yet fast for its role, and it carried a big offensive punch with bombs and machine guns. However, it was ill suited to a new role as a night fighter. The P-70's performance was degraded after it was equipped with a radar observer position in the aft part of the fuselage, four forward-firing 20mm cannons in a belly pack, and the multitude of protruding antennae needed by the SCR-540 radar, but it was wartime, and it had to do.

So the USAAF had an aircraft, ill suited as it was to do the job. Now it needed crews to fly those aircraft. Flying at night requires the same skill set as day flying, plus the ability to fly combat while on instruments. The pilot of a day fighter like the North American P-51 Mustang or Republic's P-47 Thunderbolt relied primarily on keen eyesight to detect and defeat the enemy while throwing the aircraft around the sky. A night-fighter pilot needed both keen vision and an analytical brain to manoeuvre his aircraft.

Night flyers differed from other wartime pilots in that only volunteers were used. For other assignments, the USAAF simply took a pilot graduating from flight school and assigned him to where there were shortages. Thus if there was a need for heavy-bomber or transport pilots, it did not matter one whit what the individual wanted, the USAAF needed him in the big aircraft and off he went. Flying night fighters was different. In addition to having the basic flying skills of his daytime single-engined compatriot, a night-fighter pilot had to master twin-engined flying, night formation flying, night gunnery, night recognition of friendly and enemy types of aircraft (except in rare instances of a full moon, most night identification had to consist of silhouette recognition with an occasional viewing of the exhaust flames of the engines, instead of the identifying insignia). Navigating at night, using and following both GCI controller directions and his own radar operator's instructions, was followed by night-landing training. A lot of information was crammed into the young pilot's head under wartime conditions!

To train such men, the USAAF set up its first night-fighter school near Orlando, Florida. At the newly established Drew Army Air Field (AAF) and several satellite airfields, the USAAF took advantage of the US Army Signal Corps electronic training base at Boca Raton. The Signal Corps concentrated its training on ground-based radar operators and technicians so the USAAF decision to locate there was a logical choice.

Starting in July 1942, the V Interceptor Command under Colonel Willis R. Taylor began its task of turning out night fighters. The first training squadron was the 81st Fighter Squadron under Major Donald B. Brummel. He began with no instructor pilots, no radar operators (R/Os), no aircraft, no radar, and no communications gear. Despite those handicaps, he was expected to turn out enough crews to man seventeen night-fighter squadrons within a year. He did, however, have a few veterans who had volunteered to fly with the RAF prior to America's entry into the war. They returned to US service and became the core of Brummel's programme.

He also sent five of his officers to England to train with the RAF in that country's established and efficient night-fighting programme. By this time, mid-1942, the RAF had established a policy of taking operational crews who had seen long service in the squadron and sending them on a 'rest' as instructors in the operational training units (OTUs) where new fledglings learned from their experiences. These 'rest tours' were often more hazardous than combat.

Once there, Brummel's pilots learned the rudiments of night fighting to take back to Drew Field. Likewise, American R/Os travelled to RAF Usworth to learn the new art of airborne interception radar (AI) and take those lessons back to Florida as well.

In drips and trickles, Brummel acquired a cadre of instructors and equipment. He eventually started training students with three Boeing B-17s 'Flying Fortresses' equipped as flying classrooms, one Douglas B-18 Bolo, and twenty-two P-70s.

The training establishment grew to include the 348th Flying Training Squadron (FTS) at Orlando AAF, which taught initial twin-engined and instrument flying. The 349th FTS at Kissimmee Field conducted transition training, introducing students to the flying characteristics of the P-70, and the 420th FTS at Dunnellon Field assumed responsibility for operational training. Later, as more training aircraft became available, the 424th FTS also taught students there. The units were organized under the administrative auspices of the Fighter Command School, Night fighter Division, AAF School of Applied Tactics.

To recruit pilot students, Brummel scoured the various flying schools, searching for pilots with twin-engined and, especially, night take-off and landing experience. When he started in 1942, the minimums required for volunteering for night-fighter training included six months' service as a graduated pilot, good night vision, instrument flying proficiency, 'extreme stability of temperament', and ability to command an aircrew. USAAF Major General William Kepner, commander of all fighters supporting bomber operations in England wrote to the night-fighter school:

> Night fighter pilots must be picked for their ability to operate at night and that means able to use a lot of instruments, and of course they must be fit and have good eyesight at night. They must have a willingness to fly alone long distances at high altitude with low temperatures. In other words they should combine all the aggressive and dogged fighting characteristics with a somewhat phlegmatic disposition that bores in like a bulldog without any other idea than getting the job done. Their courage and resourcefulness will have to exceed, if possible, all that any pilot has ever had before. This is some guy and you have to produce him.

The first students for the burgeoning school came from the 50th Fighter Group, Selfridge Field, Michigan. Twenty-seven volunteers left for twin-engined transition training and then went to the night-fighter school in Florida where they started training in August 1942. Once there, they flew a total of 154 hours in two areas, night flying and then night combat. Intermixed with the flying were hours and hours of ground school. Subjects covered included instrument flying (for obvious reasons!), navigating at night – it is much harder to find your way about when the world outside the window is dark and forbidding than if you can see roads, rivers and other features available during daylight – searchlight coordination, aircraft identification and an introduction to ground-control radar and airborne radar systems.

Because of the need for more night-fighter pilots, however, the requirements were eventually relaxed and as long as a man could pass through the programme, he went into night fighters.

After a painful, evolutionary process, the Army Air Force built a well-run night-fighter programme in Florida. The syllabus shook itself down into a fairly standard format of ninety-three hours of instrument flying, ninety hours of simulated instrument training in the ubiquitous Link instrument trainer, fifteen hours of night interception practice and ten ground-controlled intercepts. After that, the pilot was considered ready for combat overseas.

One of the first 417th pilots, Rayford 'Jeff' Jeffrey describes his experiences:

> I was in the last class of sergeant pilots. I enlisted in late 1939 for a couple of reasons. One, Germany invaded Poland and I thought we'd soon be in it, and two, my dad, being a sharecropper, wasn't a wealthy man. He carried me to Florence, Alabama, about 12 miles away in a wagon so I could enlist.
>
> I wanted to be a mechanic so I joined up, went to airplane engine mechanic school at Chanute in Illinois, then got stationed to Maxwell Field back in my home state of Alabama as a crew chief on North American T-6 'Texans'.
>
> It was there that a pilot, checking out my airplane for a night flight asked if I wanted to go. I said 'Yes, sir!' and grabbed a parachute and away we went.
>
> While we were flying, he asked if I wanted to fly. I was scared to death but said 'yes'. From that moment on, I was hooked and had my heart set on becoming a pilot.

Later on, now down at Tyndall Field in Florida, I was a staff sergeant and learned of the Army's sergeant pilot program. I sent in my application and held my breath. I made it in early 1942 and started down at Kelly Field in Texas for my pre-flight.

From there, I did my primary training at Stanford, also in Texas, to Sherman for basic and wound up back at Kelly for advanced flying training.

During the upper class section of advanced, they put a list of duty assignments and locations on the bulletin board for the students to choose from. I volunteered for night fighters and after winning my wings in November 1942, wound up down in Kissimmee as one of the early students, flying the P-70.

Then in January 1944 as the P-61 became available for training, the Army Air Force decided to move the entire night-fighter training apparatus west to California. Under the command of the 4th Air Force and the 319th Wing, training was reorganized into three phases: familiarization training at Bakersfield Municipal Airport; day/night interception training, where a pilot and R/O were first paired up to learn the art of night fighting at Hammer Field outside Fresno; and advanced training, which included hours of night flying at Salinas Field.

'Dirty' Dalton earned his wings by February 1944 and had done well enough to qualify as a fighter pilot. His talent almost worked against him since he was such a good pilot. The needs of the service were paramount and he was almost assigned as an instructor pilot instead of the fighter that he had dreamed of. 'However, they offered me a way out if I volunteered for night fighters. Since it was a way into combat and still said "fighter", I jumped at the chance!' he recalls.

Jim Van Voorhis recalls his journey into a night-fighter cockpit:

I graduated high school in the San Fernando Valley in May 1943. I went to the closest Army Air Forces recruiting office, which was down in Long Beach.

Now, you have to remember, at that time the draft was grabbing everyone physically capable of serving, so if I wanted a chance to fly, I had to get into the Air Force quickly or risk toting a rifle somewhere.

I took a series of tests and a physical and the recruiter told me they'd let me know. Desperately, I told him my status that if I didn't get in that day, I had a draft board notice to show up the next day. He told me to stick around and they enlisted me late that afternoon. I beat the draft by one day!

After that, they sent me to a college at St Cloud, Minnesota, for an abbreviated semester of physics, mathematics, meteorology, and the like. It was there that my group received its only form of 'basic training'. You know, learning how to march, how the Air Force was organized, etc. We were there for about three months.

Indeed, General Arnold and his staff realized that taking young kids essentially from school might not give them the best preparation for learning the numbers and maths-intensive art that is flying. Colleges and universities around the country enlisted in the war effort and played host to tens of thousands of students who wound up manning American aircraft. The US Navy had a similar programme for its future aviators.

Continues Van Voorhis:

I did my primary school at 'Tex' Rankin's Aeronautical Academy at Tulare, California. There I flew Waco biplanes. That took another three months.

Then it was off to Lemoore, California for the basic course. I flew the Vultee BT-13, the 'Vibrator' for yet another three months before heading to the last part of pilot training, the advanced course. It is during that course, you indicated what kind of aircraft – single engined or multi – that you wanted to fly.

I went to Luke Field near Phoenix for advanced; flying the [North American] AT-6 Texan and while I was there the Army Air Force brought in a P-61, the Black Widow, as a recruiting tool to try and get some of us to volunteer for night-fighter training. I really liked the look of that aircraft, all black and menacing, so I took their bait. Out of my entire class, only one other guy also volunteered.

Incidentally, I graduated from Luke, earned my wings and was commissioned as a second lieutenant one year almost to the day from graduating high school. Not too bad for a guy just turned nineteen.

Since night fighters were two-engined beasts, the Air Force sent the newly minted pilots to transition training bases where they learned to operate multiple throttles and the added complexity that a multi-engined aircraft brings to the sky.

> I went up to Mather Field outside Sacramento to check out in B-25s before being sent to a P-38 training base in Oklahoma City. Guess the training pipeline was getting full because we didn't use P-38s as night fighters. [The USAAF did eventually use one version of the Lockheed P-38, the 'M' as a night fighter but not until mid-1945 and none ever saw operational use during the war.]
>
> Anyway, I got about six flights in the Lightning before I got orders to report to Douglas, Arizona, for 'further movement on', as the service called it then, as a B-25 pilot, to Europe. Was there for several weeks, sweating out being sent as a bomber pilot before they unsnarled the problem and sent me to Hammer Field.

Dalton, a few months ahead of Van Voorhis in the training pipeline, also checked out in the A-20. Unlike Van Voorhis, however, all of Dalton's time had been in single-engined trainers. It was quite a step up in performance from the AT-6 to the A-20. Indeed, the A-20's Wright R-2600 Double Cyclone engines developed nearly 1,600hp each, almost three times the power of the AT-6's 600hp Pratt & Whitney radial.

> That was a big step up for a new pilot with less than 300 hours, but wartime created a sense of urgency so my transition was merely routine in those days. Next I started interception training, working with an R/O and learning to fly using both GCI and the R/O providing me vectors to get me into gun range of a target aircraft.
>
> We used the P-70 in this stage of training. It was a big airplane but pretty steady to fly. The tricycle gear made it a cinch to land and taxi. Learning to fly with an R/O and follow his control was interesting, much more mentally absorbing than day flying.

By August, Dalton had finished his training and found himself on the way to France to join up with his operational unit, the 417th Night-fighter Squadron. It was on a troopship there that he acquired the nickname that would stay with him for the war. Indeed, at squadron reunions, most of his compatriots only know him as 'Dirty' Dalton, so named after a cartoon strip of the time. The fictional 'Dirty' Dalton character wore wide fur chaps and an enormous 10-gallon cowboy hat pulled low over a usually tobacco-stained bushy mustache.

Van Voorhis, meanwhile, remembers:

> When I got there, there were no P-61s ready yet for students. The instructors didn't want to count my multi-engine time in the B-25, saying it wasn't a single-place ship and they didn't even look at my P-38 time so I checked out in the Douglas A-20 Havoc. The A-20 was a big sturdy aircraft; had a nose wheel like the P-38 did instead of the tail wheel that every-thing else I flew had. Much easier to land an airplane with that kind of landing gear instead of a tail dragger.
>
> After that phase was done, they had some P-61s ready for student instruction. I teamed up with an R/O who was about 6ft 7in. How he fitted in that rear compartment I'll never know!

The first U.S. R/O is generally considered to be Captain Leonard R. Hall. His piloting experience combined with an electronics background made him a perfect fit to develop the new warrior skill of R/O. Being an R/O took a different set of skills than piloting. Although the R/O did fly in the aircraft, he was not a pilot. Instead, he had to develop an almost split personality.

By using a radar scope (in fact, the early radars actually had two scopes, one displaying a 'blip' on a scale that measured altitude and another that displayed it in azimuth or 'left or right' of the fighter's nose), the R/O had quickly to picture and understand the changing geometry between the target and the fighter. He had to relay that information concisely to his pilot, in effect painting a verbal picture of what was happening. He had to instruct the pilot which direction, altitude and speed to fly in order to place the night fighter in an advantageous position relative to the target. All this happened in an almost detached way when the

R/O was effective in his job.

The other side of an R/O's role was that he was trying to shoot down an enemy aircraft that would like nothing more than to shoot down the fighter; thus he was intimately involved in the chase's outcome.

The first R/O students selected were enlisted men, mainly graduates fresh from the US Army Signal Corps's radar and radio schools. These men were hand picked from a large group of volunteers based upon their academic aptitude during their technical schooling, their high physical standards, and their background security check.

Unlike pilots, who were commissioned upon graduating, the Army Air Force at first considered the R/O to be an adjunct to the fighter, like that of a gunner to a bomber. Initially, he was not considered absolutely essential to the night fighter's success. This reasoning soon changed under wartime experience.

Future 417th members Jack Christensen, John Clemmons, Dan Cordell, Marvin Hall, Robert Hamilton, and Howard Kohrman graduated from R/O school as privates as did numerous others. George F. Allen, Joe D. Draper and Joseph M. Van Laecken reached the stratospheric rank of corporal before graduating as R/Os.

The fledgling R/Os, besides the aviation training, endured the common drudgeries of most junior enlisted men. Men were assigned daily to various menial tasks around the developing base. Some went to peel potatoes and wash dishes as kitchen police (KPs); some cleared stumps and cut brush for new areas on the ever-expanding Kissimmee location; still others worked as messengers and runners for various headquarters offices.

One of the earliest class of R/Os did not even have a formal wings-pinning ceremony as was the tradition for most other airborne trades. The men, still in their fatigues, were simply summoned into formation, called forward one at a time and presented their observer wings. The men then saluted, stepped back into ranks and after the last man was called, reported back to whatever duty they were involved in that day.

One of the first of the 417th's R/Os, Joe Draper, recalled that the training was so top secret that his father wrote him a letter asking him, 'What in the world have you gotten into?' After the younger Draper started his training, the FBI sent an agent to his hometown of Conway, North Carolina, to do a background check on him. He was unable to tell his father of his activities other than to reassure him that all was well. Radar had a top-secret priority and the operators and technicians to this day sometimes have difficulty bringing themselves to talk about it, such was the seriousness of the secrecy drummed into them at the time.

Like most wartime training, R/O training became a bit more organized as time progressed. R/O Thomas Hart of the 417th remembers:

I went through R/O training in the spring of 1944. I had washed out of pilot training and was hanging around in the 'wash-out pool' while they figured out what to do with us. They said they could take a couple of us into night fighters as something called an R/O. That sure sounded better than being a bomber navigator or bombardier which were my other options as an aviation cadet, so I said, 'Sure, I'll take it.'

So off to Boca Raton I went for R/O school. My class started in mid-March of 1944. We graduated the same day as the Normandy invasion, June 6, 1944.

In between arrival and graduating, we had pretty intensive classes on radio waves, cathode ray tubes [the 'scopes'], and mathematics. We studied the SCR-540, or Mark IV as the Brits called it, radar set. That was the one we started the war with. Later, we got the SCR-720 [RAF Mk VIII] which was much better at seeing stuff at low level.

Anyway, we also did a lot of practical, hands-on training with the equipment. We'd fly in the back of a [Beechcraft] AT-11. They had an R/O's station set up in the back that was blacked out so you could practise during the day and still see the equipment. We'd go up in pairs and practise conducting intercepts against the other aircraft, then they'd practise against us.

Most of our instructors were British civilians with some RAF types mixed in. They had a wealth of operational experience that they shared with us in the lessons. Really pretty good training for us.

We used a set of standard instructions when directing the pilot on placing the aircraft to intercept the 'bogey'. For example, we'd direct 'Increase 10' if we needed the pilot to speed up, 'Back 10' if he was closing too fast. For azimuth corrections, we'd say something like 'Gently port' for a 10 degree left turn. If we needed a harder turn, we'd say 'Hard port.' Altitude changes were handled by simply saying 'Up 500' or 'Down 1000.'

This was quite a difference from the almost self-taught R/Os of the first classes a year before!

Hart continues:

From Boca, we won our wings and went out to Hammer Field, California, for our operational training; being teamed up with a pilot and learning about the P-61.

The 'crewing up' process was pretty unique. About once a month, the night-fighter school would throw a cocktail party at the Hammer Field Officers' Club and have the latest bunch of student pilots and R/Os there in kind of a mixer. Then it was up to you to find someone you wanted to fly with. You'd each be sizing up the other guy to see if you wanted to fly with him or not.

I first teamed up with a pilot named Ray Pere, but I caught a case of poison oak shortly after while camping and was grounded for a while. Ray had to find another R/O and continue his training, so I was back stuck without a pilot.

I went to several of these parties before I found someone that interested me. Sounds funny I know, but that's how it was then. So I picked pilot George Aubill who arrived late and he picked me, so away we went for operational training in the P-70, followed by the P-61.

Aubill and Hart had several harrowing experiences while in training, that could have killed them before ever seeing the combat theatre. In one, while gaining hours in a P-70, still used as a way for students to gather flight experience, they came within a spark of being human torches. One of the fuel tanks in the P-70 was located in the fuselage 'hump' between the pilot up front and the R/O towards the tail. On this flight, the fuel tank cap was not secured and blew off during flight. Such were the aerodynamic forces that the P-70's slipstream acted as a suction pump and pulled raw aviation gasoline out, streaming it down the fuselage and into Hart's station, forming pools.

Aubill turned back to base and made a very gingerly landing, switching off everything as he rolled down the runway. The slightest spark from a switch's contact or a stray volt of static electricity would have made the P-70 and the student flyers disappear in a greasy cloud of black smoke. After the aircraft coasted to a stop, Aubill and Hart jumped out and ran, letting the base fire department deal with the fuel-soaked aircraft.

The aim of all this training was to send a trained crew to a night-fighter squadron so that it could deploy overseas and fight. It was for this purpose that the 417th Night-fighter Squadron was formed.

CHAPTER 3

Getting at the enemy is the whole purpose of a fighter squadron. Naturally, pilots – and in the case of a night fighter, R/Os – were at the tip of the spear. Backing up the aircrews was a self-contained organization capable of repairing the aircraft, fixing the radar and radios, loading and maintaining the weapons, feeding the men, medically treating them, paying them, moving them from one field to another, and a myriad of other functions, all crucial to the organization as a whole.

The organization, however, is made up of men. In the 417th's case, these men started arriving on 4 March 1943, nearly two weeks after the official order creating the squadron was given. Thirty-eight men arrived at a bare patch of ground where they were expected to begin a squadron. 'Rough' does not begin to describe the conditions at Kissimmee Field that spring in 1943.

In the heart of the Florida sand-scrub flatland surrounding Orlando (no Mouse Empire or other attractions in those days!), Kissimmee was the 'Cow Capital of Florida'. No prepared grounds or barracks awaited the new arrivals, just a patch of ground recently cleared (by the first classes of enlisted R/Os, mind you!), rough and filled with stumps and holes. It was good enough to pitch tents, so that they did. The early arrivals did not know it, but with a few brief exceptions, they would be living 'under canvas' for the rest of the war.

On that day, one of the most important men in any squadron arrived at Kissimmee. Master Sergeant Charles 'Doc' Hockman, the squadron's first sergeant, arrived to set up the framework of the unit. The first sergeant was the enlisted man responsible for maintaining the discipline and effective organization of a military outfit. He reported directly to the commanding officer and was the commander's adviser on enlisted issues. So, he was responsible for carrying out the policies and directives of the commander towards the enlisted men, but he also serves as their advocate.

First appearing in the seventeenth century in Frederick the Great's Prussian army, the first sergeant has been a fixture of the American military since George Washington's days. Indeed, the man who trained Washington's army, Prussian general Baron Von Steuben, in writing his *Blue Book of Regulations*, outlining the duties of each type of non-commissioned officer (NCO) in the Army, expended the majority of his efforts on the duties of the first sergeant. The conduct of the troops, their precision in obeying orders and the regularity of their behaviour would 'in large measure, depend on the first sergeant's vigilance.' He must be 'intimately acquainted with the character of every soldier in the company'. A poem from the US Army's past describes a first sergeant thus:

> FIRST SERGEANT'S CREED
> The first sergeant marches at the rear
> to urge on those who faltered
> Insuring none falls behind
> lest the force's strength be altered.
> The Commander positioned out in front has the glory
> Of one who leads but ne'er forget who's at the rear
> Taking care of each troop's needs.
> The cadence comes forth loud and clear
> So inspired the march won't stop
> They know who's watching over them
> the one they call 'top'.

So it was with Doc Hockman. In every reference to him in official histories, personal letters home or interviews, the men of the 417th universally held him in great esteem. Paul Peyron, in his self-published memoir of his time in the 417th, *C'est La Guerre*, described Hockman in those early days of forming the squadron,

> The first sergeant, Doc Hockman, was in charge. He was ramrod-straight, in fact he tilted slightly to the rear; and he had a booming voice. When you were called to attention, you realized you were being called by a master.
> We, the enlisted men, were his 'boys,' so we were always

taken care of, regardless of the situation.

The 'situation,' at the beginning of March 1943 was hectic to say the least. With the order to set up the 417th, a constant stream of men and material began arriving at Kissimmee. On the 6th the commanding officer, Captain Joe T. Ehlinger, a pilot who had been in the service only a few years, assumed the reins. Building a new unit from scratch is a daunting task for any officer; much less a man only in his early twenties, but the 417th was only the fourth specially designed operational night-fighter squadron in Army Air Forces history. The other three, 414-416 Night-Fighter Squadrons (NFSs), were all being built at the same time, so it was not like there was a book of 'lessons learned' that Ehlinger could consult to solve the myriad of problems he faced. Instead, he and his initial cadre of troops had to make it up as they went along. Fortunately, for him and the squadron, this cadre was comprised of experienced men who could build the squadron using the many brand new troops arriving from various technical schools around the country.

To run the aircraft maintenance side of his squadron, Ehlinger received Master Sergeant Earl Wetherald, another of the 'old timers' to serve in the 417th. Peyron, who first met Wetherald in 1942 while a private first class working as an engine mechanic and crew chief of Douglas-built A-20s and North American B-25s at Will Rogers Field in Oklahoma, was hand-picked to accompany him when he received orders to the 417th.

Peyron says of him, 'He was about forty-five years old, a World War I veteran and our squadron maintenance boss.' Wetherald became the line chief for the squadron, responsible for ensuring the servicing and maintenance of the aircraft and associated systems like the radar, the weapons and all the maintenance shops and personnel that supported those efforts.

Even though an officer, First Lieutenant Kenneth Campbell, was later assigned as the Engineering Officer, Wetherald ran the flight line activities and made sure his people turned out quality aircraft for the aircrews. Nobody wanted something he did – or failed to do – to be the reason for one of the aircraft and its crew not making it back to base.

To help him with that task, Wetherald had three flight chiefs who supervised the upkeep and care of three or four aircraft each. These flight chiefs were Master Sergeants. Elza Swain, Robert Perry and Wayne 'Mac' McMiniment. Each flight chief, in turn, had a crew chief assigned to each of the squadron's aircraft. The crew chief 'owned' the aeroplane; the crew just 'borrowed' it to go flying. The crew chief was responsible for everything related to his aircraft, from nose to tail. If it was something he couldn't fix himself like, say, the radar, then he would hound the radar maintenance people until the problem was fixed. Likewise, for reloading or replacing one of the four 20mm cannons or six .303 machine guns carried by a Beaufighter. The crew chief might not replace a cannon (although he probably knew how and could in an emergency!), but he made sure the armourers stayed on top of the plane's weaponry.

The initial group of 417th crew chiefs included Peyron, Roy Hedrick, Jennings Blankenship, Jr, Lorenzo Peters, Lewis Miller, Earl Hissett, Afton Kosick and Richard 'Big Deal' Neel. Since in the Air Force's logic the position of crew chief called for the specific rank of technical sergeant Private First Class Peyron was immediately promoted to one grade below technical sergeant, staff sergeant. After serving a minimum time as a staff sergeant, he and the other crew chiefs could sew on the five stripes of a technical sergeant.

Although a crew chief did not fly as part of his normal duties, whenever the squadron moved permanently or deployed to a location for a while, he would throw his tools and the most commonly needed spare parts in his aeroplane and accompany the crew to the new location. That way, he could keep the aircraft operational until the rest of the squadron arrived. This operation happened numerous times during the life of the 417th.

Along with the aircraft maintenance men came cooks, led by Staff Sergeant Richard Hoverson, a medical detachment of ten medics under the auspices of flight surgeon First Lieutenant Arthur Katzberg, radar maintenance men like Sergeant Carroll Poole, armourers under Second Lieutenant Herman Doescher, ordinance men under Second Lieutenant George Moeser, two intelligence officers, a weather officer, two communications officers, seventeen other pilots besides Captain Ehlinger, eighteen of the new R/Os, a supply lieutenant, First Lieutenant Rowan

Williams and his men, the squadron adjutant, Second Lieutenant J.D. Brown and his personnel staff, four GCI radar controllers, led by First Lieutenant Alpheus Withers, transport men, chemical warfare specialists, and the other specialities needed to make a squadron a completely self-contained unit, dependent on no one else in order to accomplish the mission of sending aircraft up to take on the enemy.

This influx of personnel, eventually comprising thirty-three officers and 235 enlisted men, occupied the rest of the month of March and most of April. During that time, the squadron owned no aircraft of its own, instead having to scrounge flying time from the host Night-fighter Division's training squadrons. Although the squadron had yet to be introduced to its wartime mount, the Beaufighter, the aircrews practised as much as they could in the P-70s of the school.

Put young men still in their late teens in high performance aircraft and some stupidity mixed with amazing flying feats is the inevitable result. Second Lieutenant Joe Leonard demonstrated both traits one day while flying in a P-70. He got into a flat spin but could not get enough airflow over the control surfaces to make them effective and recover. Thinking quickly, he popped the aft opening escape hatch over his head. This slab-shaped piece of aluminium and plexiglass tucked the nose under just enough for the P-70 to go down in a more conventional dive. From there, recovering from the spin was routine. Of course, Leonard spent the rest of that flight trying to get the damn hatch closed!

Another favourite flying pastime was to 'buzz' sailing boats on the nearby Banana River. By going low enough, the pilots could send the massive propwash, or turbulence, created by the P-70's engines into the sails of any unfortunate boat and tip the craft on its side. Luckily, the sailing folk could never see the numbers painted on the sides of the flat black makeshift fighters to report the antics.

Despite these events, the 417th did not have any casualties while in training. They would not be as fortunate as they headed overseas.

On 26 April 1943, the squadron loaded its gear and the men onto a train bound for Camp Kilmer, New Jersey, *en route* for 'further deployment' according to their orders.

They were heading for Great Britain for training in their soon to be acquired operational aircraft, the Bristol Beaufighter, before seeing combat.

CHAPTER 4

The 417th fell in for its last roll call in the United States on the evening of 6 May. Standing in squadron formation, First Sergeant Hockman barked each man's last name and they responded crisply with their first name and initial. After this roll call, the squadron marched to the train station and got off in New York City's harbour for their overseas transport.

In the week between arriving and marching off, the squadron had one last chance to sort its gear, qualify on various small arms weapons, get teeth and physical maladies remedied, and have a few nights in the 'Big Apple' for some last-minute fun.

It was during a session at the rifle range that crew chief Earl Hissett acquired the nickname that he would carry for the rest of the war. Indeed, at the 417th's reunions held periodically since the end of World War II, many of the veterans only knew him by this name.

He and several friends had been playing poker for three nights running. On the morning that he had to qualify on the M1 carbine, he was among the first to shoot. Finished, he sought a place to catch up on some sorely needed sleep. Finding one of the trucks that had brought the group to the firing range, he made himself comfortable and nodded off. Armament officer First Lieutenant Herman Doescher found the snoozing private and woke him up with a start. 'You sleepy sonofabitch! Don't ever sleep during duty hours again or I'll have your ass, now get back out there!' Thus it was that 'Sleepy' got his new name.

Soon, however, it was all serious business with the task of getting onto the ship that would take them to the United Kingdom, the *Queen Elizabeth*. The largest ship in the world, she could hold more than 18,000 men in her unglamorous wartime role. Because she was so large, she could not dock on the New Jersey side of the Hudson River near Camp Kilmer. Instead, the squadron had to board a ferry for a one-hour trip to the ship. Once alongside, the massive vessel dwarfed anything any of them had ever seen. They marched in assigned order up the steel gangplank into the drab, grey-painted ship. Gone were her ornate fixtures and colourful, art deco trappings. All was stripped bare to make the maximum amount of room to carry thousands of troops to destinations beyond the horizon.

Being the last ones to load, the 417th found itself up on the top deck. This was actually a blessing because the poor souls deep in the bowels of the ship were packed in like sardines, with little chance of breathing fresh air. Even the top deck was crowded to the gills. Men and equipment occupied every square inch of space. The enlisted men were bunked thirty to, what had been in peace time, a first class cabin, while the officers 'luxuriated' in only having fifteen men to a room. Unfortunately, owing to the sheer number of souls aboard, the rooms changed occupants every night. Those lucky enough to sleep indoors the first night had to give way to a not so fortunate group the next while they hunted for whatever space on deck they could find.

Paul Peyron recalls:

The night it was our time to sleep outside, Peters, Neel, Resnick and I located a spot on the deck that had walls on three sides and an overhang for cover. We threw all our blankets together and got all our gear, and made this our home for the remainder of the trip.

Eating aboard a ship with that many stomachs to fill was also an adventure in logistics. To quote the 417th's official squadron history:

The officers ate in the spacious dining salon. The men in one of the many galleys. It was a British ship. The organization was admirable and the service and food in the dining salon for the officers very good. In the enlisted men's mess it was adequate and the men survived despite having to wash their mess kits in luke warm seawater.

Peyron also spoke about this aspect of the voyage:

> I got into the chow line on the stairs that went round the
> elevator shaft. The ship had ten decks, and the mess area was
> on the lowest deck. We had to go down the stairs three
> abreast when it was time to eat. This was my first try at
> Limey food, and I was not impressed in the least when the
> fishy smell came up the stairwell shaft.
>
> After a couple of hours we made it to the mess hall, where
> we were served fish and some greens. The odour in the area
> wasn't good for your appetite and we all realized pretty
> quickly that once a day was about all we would be able to
> take.
>
> Thankfully, the ship's canteen had an unlimited supply of
> chocolate bars – Hershey and Nestlé – and we all bought them
> by the carton and lived mainly on them. I don't remember
> now, but diarrhoea or constipation must have been a problem
> during the trip.

The squadron's official history stated:

> We could buy American cigarettes on board at five cents a
> package, and everyone bought whole cartons of Hershey and
> Nestlé bars. No liquor or beer for sale, and but an occasion-
> al soft drink for those who could sweat out the line. A few of
> the more far-sighted officers had come prepared, however, and
> even shared what they had with some lucky Army nurses and
> Red Cross workers. A dull time was NOT had by all.

Finally, on 11 May, the green hills of Scotland appeared but the
ship was so packed with humanity that it was the next day before
the 417th escaped its nautical purgatory for Scottish soil. This
first overseas landfall was bittersweet for many; exciting because
it was the start of a great adventure and the first time most of the
men had been in another country, but a touch fearful because
each man had to ask himself if he would ever see home again. For
flight surgeon, 'Doc' Katzberg, it was especially poignant because
his daughter was born two days after arriving. He would not see
her for nearly two years.

The 417th and its sister squadron, the 416th, had travelled

together. Their older sibling squadrons, the 414th and 415th, had arrived in the UK several weeks earlier. Following the procedures those squadrons pioneered, the 417th split into several groups to train with their RAF counterparts in the night-fighter business for the next two and a half months.

The pilots and headquarters staff went to Twinwood, near the RAF air base of Cranfield. There the pilots would have to master the Beaufighter, which the RAF had been using since 1940 as a night fighter. The Beaufighter was always considered a challenge to fly. That difficulty was magnified by the US pilots having to unlearn techniques they had acquired while using the US-made P-70, which both the US Army Air Force and the RAF considered unsuitable for combat in Europe.

The 417th's official history does not go into the detail that another squadron's, the 414th, did, but the latter reported on the difficulties experienced in learning to fly the new model aircraft:

This transition was made exceptionally difficult and unusually dangerous because of the widely different characteristics of the two aircraft. The technique of handling the tricycle geared P-70 is much more easily mastered than is that of handling the conventionally geared Beaufighter, which requires constant attention to the controls during the entire take-off and landing operations. The slightest pilot error at these times results in a ground loop [aircraft mishap on the ground, generally results in a scrapped wing tip at best and a failed landing gear or "undercarriage" at worst]. The location of the gas line on Beaufighter aircraft presents a further hazard when such an accident occurs. Situated at the rear of the engine and forward of the fuel tank, the line is invariably broken when the ship's undercarriage collapses. Fire and explosions are the all too frequent results.

On the day that British pilots commenced to train air crews of the 414th Night-fighter Squadron, experienced aviators of the Battle of Britain admitted without exception that the Beaufighter was the most difficult of all British aircraft to fly.

The British made their program as comprehensive as was humanly possible, and undoubtedly employed additional patience in their efforts because these trainees were

Americans. However, by comparison to British trained crews, the conversion problems of the 414th were multiplied many times. To effect the conversion from the P-70 to a Beaufighter, a pilot had to unlearn more habits and learn more new techniques in flying them than would have been the case in changing to any other airplane. It was necessary for them to master a new engine completely foreign in both design and operation. The airframe was vastly different in construction, balance and airfoil characteristics from that of any aircraft they had flown in the United States.

One of the first and most vivid problems faced by pilots of the 414th [and 417th when they came through] was the use of thumb-controlled brakes in place of toe brakes. From the first day these pilots had stepped into an Army airplane to the day they entered a Beaufighter, they had used the toe brake. They had to forget their first flying habit and master a new coordination. They were obliged to understand the Beaufighter airframe thoroughly in order to keep from unduly straining the gear, empennage, and controls in taxiing, taking off, landing and maneuvring in combat. They could not taxi with the ease they had formerly used because the Beaufighter had slick tires, airbrakes, and a heavy tail that would whiplash at the slightest laxity in control.

Handling the throttles and getting maximum performance from the sleeve-valved Hercules engine required a complete change in conception of control for American trained pilots. The increase in inertia within the engine, the lag in response to the throttles and the cooling of this differently cowled engine all offered new problems. On take-off they had to start the runway straight and use throttle control because the rudder was not effective until the Beaufighter attained sixty miles an hour; in other words, rudder control required not only anticipation but intuition.

After becoming airborne the speeds of the Beaufighter and the P-70 compared favorably. However, the lag between control surface pressure and reaction was greater in the Beaufighter. Because Beaufighter trim controls, particularly rudder and aileron, were much less sensitive than those on a P-70, the former seemingly could never be trimmed to fly 'hands off.' Although the facility of the Beaufighter in maneuvring in combat would later be appreciated, American pilots beginning to fly this craft felt they did not have full control of the ship and were ill at ease. A common feeling among nightfighters, which resulted in the transfer of some men back to American equipment, was expressed by a pilot of 250 combat hours when he stated that only during his last twenty hours did he really know that he had the Beaufighter 'all buttoned up.'

Royal Canadian Air Force (RCAF) pilot, Major General Bill Vincent, then a pilot officer (equivalent to a US second lieutenant) recalls seeing some 'Yanks' at his airfield during that time.

I was with 409 Squadron [RCAF], an operational unit in the UK. When the Americans came in, the RAF didn't want to clog up their training pipelines with all these 'sprog' Yanks, so they farmed them out to several operational squadrons to be brought up to speed.

As I was just a P/O, I didn't have much to do with training them, but our flight commanders and deputy flight commanders did most of the flying training for them.

The 417th had its share of difficulties in the transitioning to the Beau and, in fact, one pilot did request a transfer out owing to his inability to master the quirky British fighter. He was replaced by Second Lieutenant Robert Swift. Swift, like thousands of other Americans, had enlisted in the RCAF in order to get into the fight before the US entered World War II. He had been an RCAF pilot for two years and seen combat before switching back to the US Army Air Forces, thus bringing some badly needed experience to the 417th.

Another pilot, Rayford Jeffrey, says of the Beaufighter:

I thought it a fine aircraft, however it had some good point sand some bad points.

First the good: the cockpit was well built and stayed together in most crashes when the rest of the aircraft was demolished. It was also the most heavily armed fighter on either side during the war.

On the bad side; the Beau would ground loop if you blinked your eyes at the wrong time or lost your concentration for a second.

For example, I was checking out a new pilot on his first flight. Since there is only one pilot's seat, the student was in the seat and I was standing behind him, looking over his shoulder. I said to him, 'See those three Beaus on the side of the runway, flat on their bellies? They ground looped on take-off so whatever you do, don't hit them.'

Now the Beau didn't have counter-rotating propellers [turning in opposite directions]. Both props turned to the left, as opposed to the P-70s whose fans turned to the right. Both propellers turning in the same direction generates a lot of torque that requires a pretty significant rudder input to counteract.

In the Beau, if you were slow on putting in that rudder, a ground loop was inevitable. Sure enough, this student is slow on the rudder and hit all three broken Beaus with our aircraft now being number four in the row.

The Beau was not noted for its single-engined operation. Any pilot who lost an engine and brought it home deserved the DFC in my opinion.

The other members of the squadron likewise had to learn to operate in, on or with the new aircraft. The R/Os, many by now commissioned as flight officers, a kind of warrant officer rank, moved to the British R/O training base called RAF Usworth. They had four hours of class a day, learning the British radar equipment installed in the Beaufighter, the Mk IV. Since the US equipment used in stateside training was based upon this very design, the American R/Os had an easier time learning the new equipment than the pilots.

The R/Os followed the class work with half a day flying in Avro Anson training aircraft. Like the AT-11s back in the United States, the 'Annie' was configured as a flying radar classroom, with an R/O station in the back where an experienced instructor could coach the neophyte American.

Engine mechanics and crew chiefs went to the same base as the pilots, RAF Cranfield. Crew chief Paul Peyron paints a picture of the Beaufighter.

The Bristol Beaufighter was a two-engined, two-crew aircraft. The engines were fourteen cylinder sleeve-valved Hercules radials. It had four 20mm cannons and six .303 machine-guns along with the radar antenna 'arrow' sticking out of the nose and the receiving antennas on the wings.

As far as the engines go, the sleeve-valve operation was a major problem. The sleeve ran up and down and turned 45 degrees between the cylinder wall and the piston. This movement opened up the intake and exhaust ports for combustion and exhaustion. The sleeve was operated with a crank arm that had a habit of breaking, causing a cylinder failure. Replacing that called for an engine change. Two hundred and fifty hours was the limit on these engines, while the poppet-type valve engines [like in the P-70] were good for 800-1,000 hours.

The magnetos were also a constant problem. We had to clean them out almost daily with carbon tetrachloride. The aircraft's skin was the thinnest possible gauge [of aluminium], and it was impossible to walk out to the wingtips – you had to crawl to prevent damage.

The wing-to-fuselage fairing screws were always backing out during gunnery firing; in fact, we had to tape them down and coat them with aircraft dope to keep them in place.

The aircraft did have some good features, however. It had the throttle and prop controls on one control so you just had a bunch of gates to slip into for take-off, climb and cruise.

Starting was simple: it had a primer in each wheel well. The pilot yelled 'Contact!' and ran two fingers in the two [start] buttons and as the blade started to turn the mechanic gave it a shot of prime from the wheel well. It never went over four blades before firing.

It had an exhaust system that came forward and under the wing, exhausting in a slotted pattern, making the exhaust hard to see at night, and causing very little noise. The Japanese called it 'the whispering death' on account of its quiet approach.

Fellow crew chief 'Sleepy' Hissett concurred. 'Those things were a wreck. Had to work on them all the time. We had to change the [spark] plugs after every mission and the magnetos about once a week. With only one assistant to help out, we were spending a lot of hours on those airplanes.'

The armourers, ordnance men, cooks and bakers and other specialists found themselves attached to various RAF units both to learn and to give the hard-pressed British a short break. 'Doc'. Katzberg found himself helping in various RAF station hospitals so that his RAF counterparts could take a short spell of leave.

Finally, on 23 May, the 417th got its first assigned aircraft. The RAF turned over twelve Beaufighter Mk VIs. In what would become a trend throughout the time the squadron depended on the British to supply Beaus, these aircraft were not new, were not in the best of shape, and in fact were other units' cast-offs. Shortly thereafter, the reassembled squadron moved to RAF Scorton for operational training as a unit. The newly retrained pilots and R/Os teamed up in the new aircraft. They flew hours and hours of practice intercept missions against each other using the many British GCI stations scattered about the country.

It was at RAF Scorton that the 417th began a long and profitable relationship with Flying Officer (equivalent to a US first lieutenant) George Parrott, RAF, and his Air Ministry Experimental Station (AMES). In US terms, this was a GCI radar station. Parrott, a phlegmatic expert at his craft, coached the 417th crews in the complicated co-ordination procedures required to prosecute a radar contact successfully. He took infinite pains in teaching the Americans to make aggressive yet smooth changes of heading and altitude while searching for the target. Often, those aggressive tactics at the beginning of a chase resulted in only minor corrections being needed in the intercept geometry at the finale, when the fighter crew was busy looking out for the target instead of wildly swinging the fighter from side to side in that last stage.

A smooth intercept resulted in the desired action: that of a quiet kill instead of a blazing gun battle if the bandit saw the fighter too soon. Part of his instructional technique was to trace what he saw on his GCI radar scope from the beginning of an intercept until the end. By marking the changing positions of the radar 'blips' at various times and noting the radio commands to and from the fighter, he could recreate the action for the crew to study on the ground. The highest praise a pilot or R/O could receive was a pencilled 'Good show!' on a piece of parchment paper filled with curving lines and cryptic radio calls. 'What a bloody cock-up!' ruined an R/O's day. Parrott was a master in this three-dimensional chess game and the 417th crews learned his lessons well.

The squadron's own controllers learned under Parrott and the other RAF instructors. Led by First Lieutenant William Williamson, these four men belonged to the 417th but attached themselves to the Signal Corps-owned US GCI units in the squadron's operating area. Thus, when a 417th crew went up, they were listening to a familiar voice and knew that the ground controller would do his best to look out for the airborne crew.

Flying Officer Parrott would later also serve with his GCI unit in the same locations where the 417th would fly combat. They would hear from him again in the future when as the crews used to say, 'You are only as good as your ground controller.' And they would be very good indeed.

They also practised some badly needed long-range navigation before heading to the combat zone. The US R/Os did not include that training in their stateside repertoire and the RAF recommended that the squadron rectify that situation since they had found under combat conditions that the Beaufighter crew was responsible for its own positioning and getting home in combat. The navigation training was also a necessary skill for the forthcoming trip to North Africa and combat.

Unfortunately, it was also at RAF Scorton that the 417th suffered its first casualities. While practising air-to-ground gunnery, the crew of Flight Officer Frank McClain, pilot, and Flight Officer Joe Hendershott, R/O, crashed while returning from the training sortie. They were also carrying mechanic Corporal Walter Dyer aboard. McClain and Dyer were killed and Hendershott severely injured in the crash. This crew was soon replaced by pilot Flight Officer Theodore 'Deke' Deakyne and R/O Sergeant Pettingill.

Deakyne was another American who had served in the RCAF and had combat experience flying fighter-bomber missions over German-occupied France in A-20s and de Havilland Mosquito aircraft. Pettingill had shipped over to the UK with the 415th NFS, but owing to illness had washed back while that squadron continued training. He recovered in time to be reassigned to the 417th.

During July 1943, the squadron had numerous promotions, including the commanding officer Joe Ehlinger, who rose from captain to major. R/Os Private Bill Roble and a Polish officer serving in the RAF, Flight Officer Thaddeus Kulpinski joined the squadron from the RAF training programme. The squadron also received orders to ship out to the exotic sounding locale of Tafaroui, Algeria. Twelve crews would fly the 1,200 mile trip while the ground crews and extra airmen would take a ship, along with all the squadron's supplies.

All twelve Beaus took off but the one crewed by pilot Roland Lehman and R/O Joe Draper developed a rough-running engine and had to turn back to their starting point, RAF Port Reith on the southern coast of England. After waiting almost thirty days to have the offending engine changed, they took off for North Africa via a fuel stop in Gibraltar. After an uneventful flight, they were still nearly an hour out when they realized that the Hercules engines were consuming fuel at a much higher rate than anticipated. They were uncertain if they would make it to the 'Rock.'

Finally, the famous British bastion poked its crown above the horizon and the crew radioed the control tower, requesting a straight-in approach due to low fuel. The tower, not expecting a lone Beau at the time, replied that the crew would have to give the 'proper signals and enter the traffic pattern to await their turn'. Lehman summed up his aircraft's predicament with a pithy, 'Then go ahead and alert Air-Sea Rescue because we are going into the drink.' His Beau quickly became number one for landing.

So dry were the fuel tanks that the engines sputtered to a halt while the big fighter was rolling down the runway. The RAF had to tow it to a parking spot.

The rest of the air echelon, led by Major Ehlinger, had arrived in Algeria and Ehlinger had put the oldest officer in the ground detachment, thirty-year-old First Lieutenant Arthur Katzberg, in charge of getting the bulk of the squadron to the right place via ship. Sixty years later, Katzberg still can relate how he was overwhelmed to learn of his responsibilities in bringing almost 200 men through the complicated process of shipping from one station to another, particularly when the commander would not reveal the destination since it was 'classified'! He says:

> I'd been drafted as a doctor and then sent to flight surgeon school. I had had a total of two weeks military training so I had no concept of military procedures and protocol. I asked Ehlinger how would I know where to unload the men and equipment and he said he'd be there waiting for us, to not worry about it.
>
> So we loaded up aboard the SS *Durban Castle* at Greenock, Scotland on 11 August and sat there until the ship sailed on the 16th.
>
> Once at sea, the senior officer on board, a British Army brigadier general would inspect the troops. I had no idea how to report to him when it came time for him to inspect our men, so I stuck my hand out to shake hands! He quickly but nicely informed me the proper way to salute a superior officer and carried on with the inspection.
>
> We sailed down the coast of Spain and Portugal and went through the Straits of Gibraltar on a beautiful moonlit night. I can still see that in my mind to this day, really a lovely sight.
>
> Anyway, we arrived at the port of Phillipville in North Africa. Well, there was no Joe Ehlinger to meet us so we stayed on board to the next stop, which was Algiers. No Ehlinger. We continued on to Oran, nobody waiting for us.
>
> The ship's captain came to me and said, 'You have to get off here, I'm going back to England and there are no stops between now and there.' I decided to keep the men on board since I had no way of knowing where the rest of the squadron was and would let the Army Air Force figure it out in England rather than risk having us stuck in some strange port with no support.
>
> So off we went for several hundred miles back towards England, then the ship got a radio message directing it to turn around and go back to Oran where we were to unload.
>
> When we got back to Oran, there was Joe Ehlinger on the dock yelling, 'Doc, I found you!' Right! But such are the fortunes of war and we made it to where we needed to be after all.

CHAPTER 5

'Doc' Katzberg and the men were taken in trucks to their home for the next five months, the airfield at Tafaroui, Algeria, about 20 miles south of Oran. A flyblown, hot, humid, alternately dusty then monsoonally wet field, Tafaroui was called by none other than General James 'Jimmy' Doolittle 'the muddiest place in the world'. The mud was most often described in letters home as 'like gumbo'.

Meanwhile, most of the crews that had flown in from England had arrived almost two weeks earlier and had started operations immediately under the tactical command of the RAF's 337 Wing. Servicing their own aircraft, using RAF messing tents and blankets, the crews began flying night patrols to counter *Luftwaffe* raids against the busy harbour and escorting shipping convoys in both day and night missions. These convoys carried men and material to the fighting now raging in Sicily and Italy itself. This schedule combined with working on their planes when not flying wore the crews to a frazzle so it was with great relief that the entire squadron came together.

Unfortunately, the very next day after this reunion, the 417th suffered its second aircraft loss. Paul Peyron, crew chief on Beau number V8856, recalls that the squadron was responsible for maintaining a two-plane patrol from dusk to dawn to safeguard Oran harbour from marauding German bombers. It was from one of these patrols that First Lieutenant Chester Watson and his radar observer, Flight Officer Tello De Santis, failed to return.

They couldn't find the field due to dense morning fog. The 417th's Beaus had no sort of homing devices on board so the crew couldn't pinpoint home. They overflew the base and crashed into the foothills of the Atlas Mountains several miles away. Soon after their crash, the squadron placed a search-light at the runway's end to guide returning crews in case of another heavy fog.

The squadron also modified a radio transmitter so that its signal could be displayed on the Beaufighter's radar. Crews could then fly home by following that signal. But ominously, two crews were gone without yet firing a shot in anger.

The 417th's young men found much to experience in North Africa. Besides the night fighters, the RAF had a squadron of Lockheed Ventura bombers for anti-submarine hunting and a rescue unit of Supermarine Walruses, an ungainly, yet immensely strong amphibious biplane. Free French forces operated in a squadron of American-donated Bell P-39 Airacobra day fighters.

The Walrus, a welcome sight to the many survivors it picked up at sea was a unique aircraft. It took off at a ridiculously slow speed, cruised not much faster, and landed even more slowly. It had a seaplane's boat hull and had retractable landing gear for land operations. It was built like a tank. In one event at Tafaroui, an RAF pilot failed to lower the landing gear and touched down. He skidded down the runway for about 50 yards, ending up in front of a group of 417th maintenance men on their flight line. When the Americans reached the cockpit, the pilot calmly said, 'I forgot, I forgot.' The 417th men jacked down the landing gear for him and without so much as looking back in thanks, he taxied away.

Besides the other military units at Tafaroui, the men had a taste of the unique blend of Arab and French culture that was Algeria. Most of the Arabs encountered were dirt poor, making a hand-to-mouth living. The GIs, as they have done in every land in every war, soon commenced bargaining with the locals for trinkets and souvenirs and on occasion even items more exotic. Peyron recounts a trip into the big city of Oran where they saw a large group of excited Arab men shouting and gesturing towards a platform. On it, daughters were being auctioned off by their fathers for the highest bid to future husbands. He says that the less generously endowed by nature never got much action, but the amply gifted drew wild bidding. Some things are just universal ...

Operationally, the aircrews kept flying, often day and night, and the aircraft took a beating from the hard use and lack of spare parts. Excerpts from the squadron's pilots' log – a record-keeping method set up by the operations officer, Ken Nelson, to help the novice pilots learn from each other's experiences – are telling as to both the condition of the weary Beaufighters and the inexperience of the joint air/GCI teams needed to make night fighters effective. Some of the callsigns and acronyms included:

Bishop XX. 'Bishop' was the squadron's radio callsign while in Africa.

XX was the unique two digit number assigned to each pilot; Nelson was Bishop 71.

NFT. Night-flying test, a day flight designed to check the aircraft and radar systems before flying it operationally that night.

PI. Practice intercept. Two Beaus flew together, one acting as a target while the other used GCI and the on-board R/O to conduct an intercept as the fighter. The aircraft took turns in each role.

R/T and/or VHF. Radio/transceiver and/or very high frequency – the aeroplane's radio.

Stalecrust/Fishbone. GCI control stations.

Bradshaw. The Tafaroui flying control tower.

Entries from this log include:

Sep 26, 1943:

Capt K. Nelson, BISHOP 71, acft # V8743, time 0930 – gunnery flight, didn't get off the ground because the right propeller was somehow disconnected from the prop pitch control. Also, same engine only put out 2600 rpm at full throttle.

2Lt George Hughes, BISHOP 62, V8743, time 1615-1625 – gunnery flight, took off, right motor vibrating excessively, landed and wrote up ship as u/s [unserviceable].

Sep 27, 1943:

FO Williamson, BISHOP 64, V8450, time 1054-1124 – took off and right engine was rough and oil pressure dropped down to 70 and fluctuated between 70-90, so landed. Found four piston rings broken. Wrote it up in [form] 1A.

Sep 28, 1943:

FO K. Fuller, BISHOP 65, V8814, time 1930-2200 – worked with FISHBONE. On take-off right cylinder head temp. was up to 285 degrees C., but not running rough. Ran 3 interceptions. FISHBONE was pretty hot. Tried one head on and it worked out ok. Got visuals at 1000ft. Upon return to field, right engine was so rough it nearly vibrated us out of the plane on downwind leg. Just before I turned on approach, right engine quit but for once I had plenty of altitude and came in with full left rudder, no trim. You can't taxi with one engine either.

Oct 2, 1943:

1Lt Joe Leonard, BISHOP 56, V8806, time 1920-2250 – took off on vector 280 for a mission with STALECRUST. Playmate with BISHOP 70. I climbed to 11,000 ft and Joe Long [the R/O] took over. Lt Long made 14 interceptions in three hours and all were good. The R/T on the starboard set was weak. The landing was lovely but somebody dropped the runway about five feet.

Oct 4, 1943:

FO Fuller, BISHOP 65, V8819, time 1915-2015. Scrambled for bogey. On arriving at airplane couldn't get a crew to start engines and had to use R/O. On take-off plane made noise that sounded like the nose had come off. Climbed at +4 [manifold pressure – a measurement of engine power] and 2400 rpm. Port radio set was out and couldn't receive on any channel. Finally BRADSHAW managed to contact me and I returned to base. Ceiling at 2,000 and lowering steadily.

Since the Beaus were RAF craft and only the four US squadrons used them, the US Army Air Forces never set up a supply system for spare parts and replacement equipment. The 417th had to beg, barter and creatively 'requisition' the parts needed to keep their planes airworthy.

The constant flying also took its toll on the aircrews. Since they had to fly both day and night missions, they never could get a solid block of time to sleep. The catnaps and short snoozes were not enough to replenish their energy and keep them alert. They finally got relief from the daytime missions from the P-39 unit, except when the weather was too bad for the single-seat craft; then it fell back on the 417th's shoulders.

Finally, in the first week of September, a 417th crew came to grips with a German aircraft. A radar station picked up enemy air activity approaching the area and vectored Second Lieutenant Jack Kirwan and Flight Officer Joe Van Laecken on night patrol in their Beaufighter to investigate. Over Oran, the crew snapped to the heading given by GCI to make the intercept and soon found themselves picking up the contact on their own radar. The radio code word for a fighter taking control of an intercept is 'Judy', a word that is still used today by the US and other air forces. Thus it was with great excitement that Kirwan radioed the GCI site, 'Judy!'

Van Laecken gave concise instructions to Kirwan to position the Beau in the best position to catch the 'bogey'. Until they could see and identify the other aircraft, they would not know if it was the enemy or not. It could potentially be a friendly aircraft just in the wrong place. So, until they laid their eyes on it, it would remain a 'bogey'.

The radar used by the Beau, as mentioned earlier, was the British Mk IV, a first-generation set. One of its limitations was its inability to see low-flying aircraft. The electromagnetic energy it transmitted travelled in all directions and kept on travelling until the waves hit something like an aircraft and a small part of the energy was reflected back. This reflection is the essence of radar. The reflection was displayed on the radar scope as a blip to the operator who then had to decipher where it was in relation to his own aircraft.

Radar maintenance technician Sergeant Carroll Poole says of the British equipment:

From an operator's perspective, the RAF radar was better than the US-made SCR-540 [a copy of the Mk IV]. The RAF gear was more sensitive to contacts down low which was where most of the Germans flew in trying to attack convoys or harbours.

Later, in an upgraded radar, the British Mk VIII, presented the target information of bearing left or right and above and below the fighter on one scope. The US version, the SCR-720, used two separate scopes to present the info. We had that set in training school. Many's the time that an R/O complained to me of having to 'keep his head on a swivel' while using the US equipment.

From a reliability and maintainability standpoint, the British equipment was a mess. Due to their urgency of needing the sets back during their dark days during the Blitz attacks in 1941 and '42, they churned those sets out as rapidly as possible. Wiring, vacuum tubes [this was well before the invention of the integrated circuit], relays and condensers were slapped into the casing anywhere they could fit it. There was no standardized placing of anything.

Troubleshooting one of those sets was a time-consuming task. You'd have to figure out what they had done on each individual set and then diagnose the problem. On the US-made sets, everything was in the same place in every radar.

Since the energy reflected back from the ground in comparison to something as minuscule as an aeroplane is massive, a huge mass of energy or 'clutter' is displayed on the scope. A blip could easily be lost amid the clutter, thus the Mk IV's inability to see targets at low level. Van Laecken had to be at the top of his game to make this intercept. The odds were that it was not a friendly, since it was flying very low and Kirwan had to open his throttles wide and dive to try and catch it. So steep was the initial dive and so hard did Kirwan flog the used Beau that he ripped a skin panel off the top of his starboard wing.

Finally, they obtained a visual and identified the quarry as a Junker Ju 88, a fast, twin-engined multi-purpose *Luftwaffe* aircraft skimming along above the waves. Most often used as a fast medium bomber, the Ju 88 also did service as a mine layer and as a night fighter itself. Definitely a match for a new Beaufighter, even more so for the hand-me-downs that the 417th flew, it was a fast, deadly adversary.

Kirwan, unable to close the gap any further, opened fire at around 700 yards, quite a long distance in aerial combat where ranges of 200-300 yards were the norm. In a perfect intercept, the fighter would close to about 100 yards before firing. That distance gave the best chance of scoring a killing hit in the first few rounds of cannon and machine-gun fire. Seven hundred yards was literally a long shot.

Miraculously, Kirwan's shots ran true. The Ju 88 staggered and smoke streamed from one of his engines. Unfortunately, the wounded plane was able to escape in the still dark night, heavily damaged but still flying. Kirwan, his own Beaufighter vibrating madly from the firing, lost speed due to the recoil from the ten weapons and the drag from the damaged right wing. Joe Van Laecken remembers that he could see down into the wing and that it was vibrating abnormally and he excitedly told Kirwin that they had better slow down before the whole wing came off!

Peyron, who mentioned earlier that the screws attaching the wing fairing to the fuselage kept backing out, flew a training mission once when the crew practised air-to-ground firing. He says, 'Holy smoke! When we fired, the vibrations were so bad I thought we stopped in the air. Now it came to me why all those screws retracted from the fairings.'

So it was that Kirwan and Van Laecken scored first blood for the 417th!

A big worry for the squadron leadership still was the desperate lack of spare parts for the aircraft. According to the squadron's records, the 417th averaged eleven aircraft assigned at any one time. Of those, eight or nine were flyable and those only through Herculean efforts on the part of the ground crews. Such was the need for parts that the newly promoted squadron commander, Major Ehlinger, flew to Algiers himself to plead his case with the combined US/British headquarters there, but to no avail.

As September slipped into October, the situation became critical. Engines designed for only 250 hours were being pushed further and further beyond that point. An engine failure in flight during a critical phase of a mission was bound to happen, and the

Beau had a very poor reputation for returning on one engine.

Lieutenant Joe Leonard of the Florida P-70 spinning incident lost the starboard engine when it broke from its mounts and twisted inwards. Besides the heavy drag and asymmetrical thrust caused by losing an engine like that, the fear factor must have been high when the propeller tips started gouging into the cockpit only inches from his foot! In a piece of skillful flying, he made it back to Tafaroui.

The squadron history recounts the following incident regarding a Beau losing an engine, but for obvious reasons does not report the pilot's name:

> Beaufighter suffered engine failure on take-off with numerous passengers on board. Pilot, going too fast to abort the take-off on runway remaining, did a skilful job of getting ship airborne and around for successful landing. Passengers, none the wiser of the close call, departed with thanks for the ride.

It is amazing how close a little showing off for a planeload of visiting army nurses came to catastrophe!

Exacerbating the parts shortages in several cases were understandable but still unbelievable mistakes made by pilots and, sometimes, crew chiefs. One pilot, also not named in the 417th's official history, lost control of the Beau while taxiing and ground looped. As we saw in Chapter 4, this was not a rare occurrence. What made this accident memorable was that he ran over a latrine, putting a wheel into the muck It is hard enough and takes considerable effort to pull an aircraft from a mud hole without adding in the latrine's 'yuck' factor!

Another Beau was damaged when the maintainers, while raising it on hydraulic jacks to work on the landing gear, made an error and it slipped off one of the jacks. The sudden drop drove the shaft of the jack clear through the wing.

On another occasion, 'Big Deal' Neel changed both engines on his Beau. He did his usual skilful job with one small exception – he forgot to put oil in before running them up. Both engines were total write offs and had to be changed again.

Once, after several days of non-stop rain, the squadron faced the unbelievable sight of a perfectly good Beaufighter lying flat on the ground. The hardstand parking spot, made of prefabricated perforated steel planks, seven simply sank into the water-saturated mud from the weight of the 7-ton Beau pressing down on it. The sad fighter had to be jacked up, drained of water and cleaned up before it could fly again.

As was common in flying squadrons of the day, the 417th acquired a squadron administrative airplane or 'hack'. This plane was used to run errands to the widely dispersed Allied airfields and for the pilots to gain additional hours' flying without taking one of the operational aircraft out of service. A hack is usually either an older aircraft that has been replaced by a newer model or one that is surplus to a unit's needs. The 417th picked up a Hawker Hurricane that the RAF no longer needed. The 'Hurri', made famous during the Battle of Britain, was by now obsolete as a dogfighter against the *Luftwaffe*'s fighters. It did still give yeoman's service as a light bomber, but only close to the front lines. The 417th was quite removed from those so this Hurricane was a gift.

Other than a pilot's manual, there was no formal training for the squadron's pilots; they had to rely on their experience and exuberance to fly the rugged little fighter safely. Just how rugged was demonstrated by one pilot who raised the tail too high during the take-off run and ground down the tips of the nose-mounted wooden propeller. Going too fast to stop before he ran out of runway, he managed to stagger the poor Hurricane into the air. Finding it still flew satisfactorily albeit a bit more slowly, he performed a fine aerobatic show over the airfield before landing. His write-up in the aircraft log that the maintainers used to fix pilot reported problems read, 'Shortened prop on take-off. No action required.'

Another 417th pilot flying the hack buzzed the operations shack. There was a radio antenna on a 20-foot pole sticking out of the middle of the tent. As in the buzzes back in Florida during training, this pilot knocked down the antenna!

These flights gave the young pilots experience and confidence in handling an aeroplane aggressively, traits they would need as operations continued.

On the evening of 22 October 1943, Ehlinger led a two-plane patrol that encountered a big gaggle of the enemy. With R/O Flight Officer Dan Cordell in his Beau and his number two crewed by the veteran First Lieutenant Bob Smith, pilot, and Flight Officer Howard Kohrman at the second Beau's radar scope, Ehlinger was directed by GCI against a mass *Luftwaffe* raid. The Germans were making a maximum-effort raid against a convoy sailing to Oran. The convoy was out to sea heading south towards landfall when the patrol, at first 30 miles away, received GCI instructions to 'buster' (push the throttles all the way forward, to go as fast as they could) and fly an easterly heading. Ehlinger's flight made radar contact and screamed in against the twenty or more blips that Cordell could count on his scope. Twenty or more against two were not great odds, but then again, the size of the enemy formation could work against them. With twenty of his own aircraft nearby, a gunner aboard one of the Ju 88s would have to make very sure he was not firing on one of his own whereas the American Beaus could safely assume that any aircraft they spotted was an enemy.

At 8,000 feet, Ehlinger saw the formation, once again down on the deck just above the waves. They were screaming eastward away from the fight and were soon lost to view in the gathering night and sea mist. Even though they did not bring the enemy to battle, the patrol did succeed in its larger mission of protecting the Oran-bound convoy.

After the scorching hot months since their arrival in Tafaroui, November brought torrential rains and cold. The mud became routinely ankle deep and worse. As the weather worsened, the squadron, by its own efforts, made great strides in improving their supply problems.

Obtaining another hack, a B-25 bomber nicknamed the 'Strawberry Roan', the squadron was able to range throughout the Mediterranean in search of Beaufighter parts. Besides the other three US Beau squadrons scattered in North Africa and Sicily, the RAF operated several of its own Beaufighter squadrons there.

Some were night fighters like the 417th, others were strike aircraft engaged in punishing German ground forces and coastal shipping. These strike Beaus were an even more fearsome than the night fighters because in addition to their ten automatic weapons the RAF had recently armed them with eight rocket rails, each capable of launching a 60lb high-explosive projectile.

These rockets were devastating against hardened ground targets and ships.

Despite the inability of the US supply system to get the 417th the parts it needed, the sheer numbers of RAF Beaus in use provided a ready source of equipment. The 417th was able to acquire spare parts and equipment through means both legal and otherwise. The RAF, on the other hand, maintained its practice of giving the Americans their cast-off airplanes when the times came to add to the US squadron's table of equipment. Aircraft were lost through accidents, combat, and just wearing out. The RAF was bound by written agreements to resupply the US squadrons with aircraft, but they did not specify the condition those aircraft had to be in!

US inspectors, on their rare visits to the squadron, were amazed at the number of overhauls and repairs made to the 417th's Beaus. If those aircraft had been American, they would have been junked! The engineering officer, First Lieutenant Kenneth Campbell, a Yale-educated Alabama boy, recalled in a letter seeing a Beau show up at the squadron that he had seen in an RAF squadron's junk pile several months earlier. The 'unofficial' B-25 pressed into service as the squadron's cargo hauler became a priceless asset to keep the battered Beaus flying.

Paul Peyron picked up the additional duty of crew chief and flight engineer of the B-25. While he appreciated the 50 per cent increase in pay that came with being assigned as a flight engineer, the extra work meant many more hours in the Tafaroui cold working on his second aircraft. However, the 'Strawberry Roan' proved her worth many times over in bringing back sorely needed parts for the squadron.

In mid-December, pilot Dick McCray had an incident in his Beaufighter that he described in his diary:

FO Johnny Clemmons and I were scheduled to fly ND 201, a Mk VI Beaufighter fitted with Mk IV radar on an evening convoy patrol, so we set up an NFT with Lt 'Grumpy' Groom and FO Hal Roth in ND 171. T/Sgt Robinson and S/Sgt Peters of the engineering section wanted to see their handiwork in operation, so Johnny and I outfitted them with chest chutes and helmets. Sgt Robinson sat on the main spar, while Sgt Peters stood on the forward cockpit hatch after it was closed.

Sgt Kosick, the crew chief, pulled each engine through six prop blades. We fired up the engines and got clearance from BRADSHAW, the RAF aerodrome control, to taxi to runway 27. That gave us about 3,500 feet of paved runway, not counting the 500 feet of steel mat which had been added to the east end.

In best Beau pilot procedure, I lined up on the runway, eased the throttles up to +8 pounds boost, pushed the wheel forward and locked my elbows. The twin Hercules purred a little louder, we accelerated rapidly, the tail came up, and we were airborne about two-thirds of the way down the runway. Select 'undercarriage UP' on the control lever, and the indicators flap in the breeze.

At about 200 feet altitude, as we crossed the perimeter taxi strip, the u/c [undercarriage] locked 'Up', a noise like an explosion came from the port engine, and flames shot out beneath the gills. With only 140 IAS [indicated airspeed] showing, I eased off on the wheel with my right hand while I hit the port feather button, port throttle closed, port CO_2 button, port mixture to idle cut-off, and port mag switch to 'off' with my left. The flames went out.

A quick twist on the rudder trim took the load off my left foot. With a little fine tuning on rudder and aileron trims, she was almost ready to fly hands off. Altitude by this time was 150 feet. With starboard throttle and pitch at maximum climb settings, she edged up to 150 IAS. I didn't want to sacrifice any of that speed for more altitude, and it was now obvious that I wasn't going to get more space between me and the ground without losing speed.

It was time to analyze the situation. We were flying reasonably comfortably level, treeless farmland and pasture in front of me, but on my right the land sloped up to a ridge ranging from 250 to 300 feet high about a mile away running parallel to my course. On the left, there was five miles of level land, then steep slopes to mountains rising 2,500 to 3,000 feet.

And the RAF Pilot's Notes say on single engine operation of twin engine aircraft, no turn into the dead engine and no turns under 500 feet.

The ridge was too high and too close to make a turn into the good engine. And I had two fellows aboard with no safety harness and no altitude to use a 'chute.

So I called BRADSHAW reporting an emergency (in case they had not been watching), requesting clearance to land as soon as possible. There was no reply.

Gingerly, I eased into a very flat, very gentle turn to port. By the time I finished the 180 onto the downwind leg, a flight from the French squadron was calling for landing instructions. After their second call, I was relieved to hear Grumpy's voice, 'Shut up and keep clear, you frogs. Can't you see 54's in trouble?'

Now there's the approach to consider. I want to avoid a belly landing if possible. But with only one hydraulic pump, the undercarriage will take longer to lower. And as soon as it starts down, here will be more drag so we'll start down too. If I use flaps, there will be even more drag as well as lift. OK, we'll do u/c first, then flaps.

I extended the down-wind leg an extra mile beyond the end of the runway, then made another very gentle turn to line up on the runway. A little over twice as far out as normal, I started the u/c down. With a little back pressure on the wheel, airspeed dropped to 120. The end of the steel mat crawled towards us. Its relative position looked good and we passed over the end with about twenty feet of altitude and the two undercarriage indicators waving black and white bars at me. I held her off as the airspeed dropped to 110. The controls were definitely mushy by now, but we got two green u/c indicators. The left wing dropped, we bounced once, and rolled down the runway.

Nonchalantly, I kept a little power on and rolled the length of the runway. I discovered there was no possibility of making a turn toward the good engine to clear the runway, so I braked to a stop and killed the engine. While my passengers were disembarking, I pulled the pin on my Sutton harness, disconnected the oxygen hose and headset leads, picked up the Form 1 from its bracket, and followed them down the ladder. That's when I discovered that any writing would have to wait until my hands stopped shaking.

With the squadron's first overseas holiday season approaching, the Germans managed to have an impact on its Christmas celebrations. On a raid on Oran one night just before the holiday, they succeeded in sinking several ships. One of them was the mail ship carrying precious letters and packages from home for tens of thousands of GIs. Among those affected were the 417th's. Although the ship was salvaged and the packages did make it eventually, not many men appreciated the salt-water flavouring in their biscuits from home. The mess section did, however, put on a fine Christmas dinner of turkey and all the trimmings to help soothe any feelings of homesickness.

Squadron Christmas cheer suffered a serious blow on the 27th. Veteran pilot Bob Swift and his R/O Howard Kohrman failed to return from a patrol. No word was received from them before their disappearance and no trace was ever found of them.

The new year of 1944 brought news of imminent changes for the squadron. Since their arrival in North Africa in mid-1943, the war had moved on and the threat to Oran's harbour was greatly reduced. First the Italian island of Sicily, then Italy itself were invaded, forcing its surrender in September 1943.

Allied headquarters had already moved all the other night-fighter squadrons to airfields closer to the action in Italy, leaving just the 417th behind as a 'just in case' squadron to guard the area. The 414th moved to the island of Sardinia on a field at Elmas and helped cover the Italian coastal areas including the Anzio beach-head. The 415th was based at Naples and did much of the night intruder work of the night-fighter squadrons during this time. The 416th also moved to the Naples area. Now the 417th was needed forward.

A small advance party departed for the newly liberated island of Corsica, birthplace of Napoleon, to make the arrangements for the squadron to bed down there. Shortly thereafter, in a move still not understood, more than a third of the enlisted technical specialists left for Corsica as well. These men would spend almost four months separated from the squadron, having little to do to occupy themselves and living in very bleak field conditions. The rest of the squadron went to La Senia airfield in the Oran suburbs. They operated there for several more months, sending detachments of aircraft onward to other airfields while maintaining their convoy and night patrols in the western Mediterranean Sea.

Unfortunately, this move did not help the quality of the available aircraft. On 20 January, Flight Officer Clarence Fuller lost an engine on take-off. The Beau crumpled into a ball on the western edge of the runway in a salt lake. Fuller died instantly and his R/O, John Clemmons died hours later in the hospital.

Before finally quitting Africa for good, the 417th scored its first confirmed kill on the *Luftwaffe* on 2 February. A Beau patrol by Second Lieutenants Rayford Jeffrey, pilot, and William Henderson, R/O, was vectored onto a 'bogey' by a ship-based GCI controller – a 'Freddie', the radio code for a fighter-directing ship. Jeffrey says of this, his first combat: 'I had been on patrol close to the Balearic Islands, Majorca and Minorca. We were returning home to La Senia and were about halfway back across the Med. when I decided to fire my 20mm cannons to check their dispersal pattern.'

The dispersal pattern was the point at which the guns were harmonized or positioned while the plane was on the ground so that when the trigger was pulled, the rounds converged at a specified point in front of the aircraft. This point was set either by the direction of the squadron commander or by each individual pilot for what worked best for him. A 150-200 yard aim point straight off the nose of the plane was the most common for many fighter pilots. Any further and the rounds started to lose energy and might not do enough damage to an enemy and any closer and the fighter ran the risk of being hit by debris if the enemy exploded in mid-air.

Jeffrey continued:

While firing at the water, I noticed the pattern was somewhat irregular, being angled low and to the left. Bill Henderson's seat was towards the tail of the aircraft behind the cannons. In fact, he had to manually charge [cock] the cannons before we went into combat.

Bill clicked in [on the intercom] and observed that we only had about twenty rounds left in each of the four cannons and that home was still a long way away. Thinking this was good advice, I quit firing.

Wouldn't you know it, about five minutes later, GCI called me up and vectored me back toward Majorca to investigate a 'bogey'. Bill soon picked up contact on his radar and started giving me headings for the intercept. It was just beginning to get daylight and I got a visual about a quarter of a mile, crossing right to left [in front of Jeffrey's Beau], at about 50 feet. I was at about 3,000 feet.

I ID'd [identified] the aircraft as a Ju 88 and started my attack on him from the rear and above him, closing in to about 300 feet behind. In the twilight of early morning, I saw the flashes from the tracer ammunition of the enemy as his turret gun opened up on me.

Jeffrey heard the metallic 'plink' as the German bullets hit his Beau and fell back to assess the damage to the aircraft. Finding it still flyable, he pressed in again to attack.

Aiming just forward of his nose, I fired a very short burst and saw hits on his cockpit and down across the wing inboard of his left engine. His left wing separated from the fuselage and the aircraft immediately rolled over to the left and dived into the water. I circled above and looked for survivors but did not see any.

In my short burst of cannon fire, I used only forty rounds, ten from each one.

Halfway home, the routine hum of my engines suddenly decreased by half and the airplane tried to roll on me. I'll be damned if the enemy fire I had seen had taken out one of my engines and those birds just don't like to fly on one! In fact, I knew of several instances of Beaufighters failing to make it back on one since the aircraft couldn't maintain altitude.

So much for a relaxing trip home; I had continually to fight to remain flying, nursing it home. After all I'd been through today, I sure didn't want to have to ditch. I managed, finally, to not only make it back to base, but bring the aircraft in for a safe, gear-down landing ... no mean feat on one engine.

A hairy day, to be sure, necessitating the medical application of a healthy dose of Kentucky's finest bourbon to smooth over the excitement. This had not only been the first victory for me, but also the first victory of the 417th Night-fighter Squadron.

'Doc' Katzberg verified that whisky was a standard-issue item for crews returning from patrols. He would meet the crews upon their arrival and after they debriefed the intelligence officer, offer them the miniature bottle that was a prized perk of flying cast-off planes on long, dangerous missions.

This victory was a nice parting gift for the squadron as they starting packing up for Corsica and more combat. They lost another Beau before they left La Senia, but luckily not the crew, on 11 February. Lieutenant John Lee was practising single engined operations near the airfield. In light of Jeffrey's return to base in that condition only a few days prior, this was a prudent exercise. Unfortunately, after feathering the starboard engine and flying along on the remaining port Hercules engine, the starboard would not start again. Lee went through the checklist to see if he had missed anything, but while he was doing so, the Beaufighter inexorably lost height. Lee was only at 3,000ft to start with so when he realized the right engine was not coming back to life he knew he had to put the plane down and in a hurry.

When his troubles started, Lee had been flying west, just crossing over the southern end of La Senia's north-south runway. He tried to make the turn to line up with the runway but failed. At about 800ft, he stalled the Beau and it dropped onto the dry lake bed that had only a few weeks earlier had claimed the lives of Fuller and Clemmons. Although it ended up a crumpled mass of aluminium, the rugged frame saved its crew's lives. Both Lee and R/O Leonard Potter scrambled from the wreckage, shaken but unhurt.

CHAPTER 6

While the flying part of the squadron carried on from La Senia, the 417th ground detachment sent to Corsica in January to set up a base lived a stark existence, not forgotten, but certainly forlorn. The distance between the two camps was so great that except for the B-25 'Strawberry Roan', there was almost no contact between the two.

Initially, the Corsican detachment sailed from North Africa to the port of Ajaccio. From there they drove across the island to the tiny town of Ghisonaccia. They cleared the area designated for them of brush and small trees, set up their tents and belongings and waited. The other squadrons at Ghisonaccia teased them about being abandoned and playing Boy Scouts with nothing operational to do.

However, the GIs, renowned for improvising, set-to to help out the flying units that were on the island. A sister US Beaufighter squadron, the 414th, flew aircraft in each afternoon from their base on Sardinia and flew from 'Guinea Snatch', as the town was nicknamed, each night to increase the area they could cover and intercept the Germans. The 417th's men helped service these aircraft while they waited for their own to catch up.

They also worked on the 'Strawberry Roan' when she landed on her weekly flights from La Senia. She carried fresh food to help supplement the steady diet of C-rations the men were subsisting on, rotated personnel out as needed and most importantly, brought mail from home.

Paul Peyron, as the 'Roan's' flight engineer, made most of these flights and saw the conditions the Corsica men lived in. He recalls that they were so bored that 'tent fever' was a real issue.

They did daily callisthenics, went on hikes, swam in a pond up in the hills near the camp, but were starved of meaningful work.

Bored young men often turn to mischief. So it was for the 417th. One day, four troops, driving a jeep up in the hills, came across a pig crossing in front of them. Spraying it with Thompson sub-machine-gun fire, they perforated it and threw it across the hood of the jeep. The owner, however, was not pleased and with wild gesticulations and loud shouting told the four GIs so. Since they were armed and he was not, he did not get very far in reasoning with the Americans, who drove back to camp and entertained all with a succulent pig roast.

Losing the battle did not mean the farmer lost the pig war, however. The day after the incident, along with several armed friends, he showed up at the airfield's headquarters demanding payment for his loss. Since the whole place knew where the 417th got the pig, the base leadership had to accommodate the farmer. Major Ehlinger had to pay up and raised hell with the men.

In February 1944, the Corsican detachment was ordered to move to Borgo airfield, on the very northern tip of the island. Why they spent so long at Ghisonaccia doing nothing and then moved in a hurry to the new location is unknown to this day, but move they did. Out of the fourteen airfields on Corsica, Borgo was the only one that did not have a dedicated aircraft type assigned to it. Bases further to the south had day fighters (P-47s mostly) and medium bombers (B-25s and B-26s), but Borgo had a hodge-podge collection of various types.

One incident recalled by several 417th veterans is the way in which their supply officer was tricked by the supply officer of the vacating squadron. Since First Lieutenant Rowan Williams was directed to set up the operation as quickly as possible, he made a deal with a day-fighter squadron which was moving to Italy. Williams traded the 417th's tents, neatly packed in shipping crates for the already erected tents of the fighter squadron. That unit's supply officer agreed and fled the scene before Williams had a chance to inspect the standing tents. They were in very poor shape – holes galore, rotted at the stress points, and generally unusable. The long-suffering ground element spent many hours making repairs to make them habitable. They never let Williams forget his poor judgement, but they made it work as always.

Corsica was very close to the fighting in Italy; in fact it was located ahead of the front lines between the Germans and the Allies. At night, the 417th could roll up the sides of their tents and watch the flashes of artillery duels on the Italian mainland. Additionally, the *Luftwaffe* was much more active here than it was over North Africa. Numerous bombing raids against the island resulted in heavy night-fighter activity.

Once established at Borgo, the stranded maintenance specialists finally had some opportunities to work on their own aircraft. Each afternoon, two 417th planes would fly in from North Africa to Borgo to fly patrols there. At the end of the night, they would leave for La Senia again, to be replaced by another pair of night-fighters.

It was during one of these forward missions that Major Joe Ehlinger found out that rank did not always have its privileges. Having scrambled earlier in the evening against a 'bogey', he was low on fuel and had to land. Unfortunately for him, the Germans were bombing Borgo when he did so. This attack was later dis-covered to be a German mistake; they were actually after a bomber base south of Borgo. Ehlinger got his Beaufighter onto the runway, toggling the handbrakes for all he was worth. Once it stopped, he sprinted for a slit trench on the side of the runway. Unfortunately, in the dark, he could not tell that it was already full. The men inside, cowering from the explosions and shrapnel whistling through the air, could. They threw him out, crying 'Get the hell out of here!' Ehlinger found other shelter to ride out the raid and never mentioned the incident. He did not have to; once they realized who it was, the men were embarrassed beyond words. Ehlinger's silence about the matter was the perfect way to deal with the situation.

Communications officer Second Lieutenant James Simpson suffered his own indignity during the same air raid. Running the tower operations at Borgo, he had set up his cot in the hastily constructed wooden tower to be near the radios so that when an aircraft wanted to land, he could respond promptly. One night an aircraft flew over, dropping high explosives on the field. Simpson, startled from sleep by the first explosions, slapped on his steel helmet. Soon the men could hear his cursing over the noise of the bombs because he had used the helmet as a sink for shaving the previous morning and it was still full of soapy water.

Meanwhile back in Africa, the 417th kept flying its patrols in that area as well. In early March, two crews, Lieutenant Ted Deakyne and Flight Officer Tony Spier, and Lieutenant Sam Hooten and Staff Sergeant Bill Roble, were detached to augment the 416th Squadron, then based near Naples. The 416th, through deaths and injuries, found itself short of Beau crews. The 417th men acquitted themselves well, scoring two victories while 'on loan'.

'Jeff' Jeffrey found March an exciting month. On the 28th, he was on convoy escort duty about midway between North Africa and Spain with wingman Captain K. K. Nelson's fighter in a loose trail formation. GCI radioed him to intercept an incoming 'bogey' then about 40 miles north-east of the convoy. Jeffrey snapped to the given heading and pushed his Beaufighter's throttles to the stops.

> My R/O, Bill Henderson, picked up a radar contact about 030 degrees for 2 miles, low. A short time later, I tallied the contact at nearly nose on, let him get abeam of me and turned into him. It was then that I ID'd it as another Ju 88 down at about 50ft above the water.
>
> The Jerry saw me then and tried to turn into me, but since I had the height advantage and could trade the height for speed, I could out-turn him and came in behind him. I closed to about 250 yards and opened fire. As I did, the Beau slowed in its tracks due to the recoil of the cannons. I had them loaded with an alternating mix of armour-piercing, incendiary and high-explosive rounds. Most of my shots missed, but I did see a few HE rounds hit him.

In the meantime, Captain Nelson had fallen behind in order not to clutter up the air situation. Combat is confusing at the best of times, so by hanging back, he let Jeffrey concentrate on the target without having to worry whether his wingman was in the way.

> As my shots hit, I noticed something being thrown from the enemy aircraft. I continued closing to about 150 yards when I heard the staccato, metallic 'plunk, plunk, plunk' of his turret gunner's return fire hitting my aircraft.

I slowed up to see how badly my ship was hit. We had lost the radar and unbeknownst to me the hydraulics. While I was taking stock, I noticed tracer fire coming from behind me! Then Nelson radioed a 'Head's up!' call as he tried to arc his fire again onto the bandit. Just as with me, the recoil from his guns slowed up Nelson, so I was back in position to shoot again.

Another 'plunk' and I felt a searing heat in my foot. I fired another long burst at the 88, emptying my cannons. I saw parts falling off the bandit, including the turret canopy of the gunner that had shot-up my aircraft.

The Ju-88 could not maintain altitude and fell into the water, sinking very quickly. I climbed up to 3,000ft to report the kill to GCI.

Jeffrey's night was not over, however.

About five minutes later, GCI called up again and gave a vector towards a large gaggle of inbound targets. By this time I had rejoined with Nelson and a pair of RAF Beaufighters had come from their neighbouring patrol area to join in. The four of us were still in the vicinity of my kill when a large force of bandits approached.

I had never seen that many aircraft at any one time. The battle was quickly joined and each Beau scrambled for its life. I heard my wingman call he was out of the fight with five bandits on his tail.

I was busy enough about then. With only ammo in my .303 machine-guns, I couldn't fire as hard as with the 20mms, but I wanted to do as much damage as I could. With this many targets, all I could manage was a squirt of fire at one airplane before having to line up on another. I eventually shot at four different aircraft before going 'Winchester' [out of ammunition]. The RAF Beaus also did some damage although neither claimed a kill.

Days later, the intelligence guys determined that I had shot down the pathfinder for the large gaggle of fighter-bomber Ju 88s that we tangled with. This pathfinder was supposed to lead the big group to the convoy we were protecting and drop a radio-tracking buoy so the others could home in on it and thus the convoy. That was what I saw him throwing out when I first fired at him.

Intelligence also said that twenty-five of the seventy attacking aircraft never returned to base. They credited the four Beaufighters for repelling the entire attack. I was awarded one destroyed and three damaged from that fight.

Jeffrey still had to get his wounded Beaufighter home over several hundred miles of cold, forbidding water. He made it back to La Senia, but once there discovered his hydraulics problem. With no hydraulic system, he could not lower the landing gear so he and Bill Henderson rode the Beaufighter in for a belly landing.

I brought the airplane in, hitting the ground hard; so hard in fact that one of my shoulder straps broke on impact and dislocated my shoulder. The propellers bent and stopped as the fighter slithered along the runway. Finally, the Beau came to a stop in a cloud of dust, dirt, and grass.

Both Jeffrey and Henderson were pulled from the wreckage, Jeff's dislocated shoulder being the worst injury between them. 'Doc' Katzberg again administered some medicinal booze to the crew and popped Jeffrey's shoulder back into place. As for the bullet that hit his foot at the beginning of the dogfight, Jeffrey says:

I discovered the round I took in my foot had only entered the thick sole of my flying boot, coming close enough to my foot to burn it, making me think I'd actually been hit. I dug the slug out and have kept it to this day, as well as a photograph of my airplane after the crash landing.

Luftwaffe activity increased against convoys, particularly those passing through the mid-Mediterranean area. Flying from bases in southern France, these marauders sank several Allied ships. A report from the 415th NFS amply illustrates the tactics used by the Luftwaffe during this time:

1. The Germans when bombing at night usually make 4 or 5 bomb runs from different angles and evidently bomb on a time schedule. Their technique seems to be a low approach toward the target, then a climb to 8,000 feet, from which

altitude the bombs are dropped, then down to the deck again and home. The exception to the rule is the Heinkel 177, which always makes a comparatively high-altitude bomb run.
2. At night we found that the enemy used reconnaissance ships before a raid. They would send in a stooge aircraft or two to attract the attention of our night fighters. In this way they tried to draw the night fighters away from their bombers. These stooge aircraft engaged in violent aerobatics to protect themselves.
3. The 'window' [aluminium foil strips designed to fool radar systems] which the Germans used was very effective against our Mark 4 radar equipment but not so effective with our Mark 8. The enemy dropped 'window' from an altitude of 3,500 or 4,000 feet and generally saturated the area.
4. The enemy apparently has radar installed in the tails of night raiders which will detect aircraft coming up on their rear. This was indicated by the way they would go into violent evasive action (climbing, diving, turning) which we could see on our radar screen. This tail radar apparently has an azimuth range which determines whether our approach is from the right or left and the German pilots made their evasive turns accordingly. Usually, they would first make a feint toward starboard and as our plane then had to make a violent turn to starboard to stay on their tail, they would quickly turn to port. It is because of this that it is believed they know the limitations of our air-borne radar.
5. The Germans tried to jam our radar by sending out such a powerful wave that our equipment 'triggered up' and we would get only dozens of jagged lines. We could hear the hum of their jamming equipment. We tried all sorts of remedies without much success, and are convinced that we will have to deal with radar jamming during the rest of the war. Often, they would try to jam our equipment then use 'window' from their ships.

To counter the threat, all night-fighting assets had to be brought to bear and thus the 417th, the last of the night-fighters still in Africa, were called upon to take on this threat as well. To do so, they sent a nightly two-plane detachment to a bare airfield near

Cape Tenes, midway between Oran and Algiers, in addition to the two sent to Corsica almost every night, and the ones detailed to patrol the western Mediterranean. This effort stretched the aircrews and ground crews alike in keeping enough planes usable.

Each hour of flight required four or more hours of ground maintenance. The conditions at the home base of La Senia were primitive enough but at least there were other workshops to handle each area. Forward-deployed aircraft put a heavy strain on the crew chiefs who accompanied them because they had to do their regular job of keeping them airworthy, but also had to reload the guns, refuel the tanks, and patch together the radios so the crew could talk to the all-important GCI sites. Sleep became just another commodity that was in short supply for the 417th.

For this new assignment, two Beaus would fly to La Passet airfield in mid-afternoon, refuel and wait for the scramble alarm to be given. Paul Peyron, crew chief for 'Jeff' Jeffrey's aircraft, accompanied his charge on one such deployment.

> There were three or four tents at the end of the runway near the aircraft where we waited out the night. If the call came in to scramble, we all sprinted for the fighters. I'd help the crew strap in and then prime each engine using the switch in each wheel well. They could be airborne within minutes of the alert.

Only three days after facing the dogfight of his life and having his shoulder dislocated, on 31 March Jeffrey and his R/O, again Bill Henderson, were lazing in the tent, fully clothed, trying to get some rest. At about 11p.m., the klaxon blared for the crew to launch. Peyron describes a comedy of errors in getting to his airplane.

> I jumped up and took off out of the tent – immediately hooking my chin on a tent rope and throwing myself for a loop. I quickly recovered and ran to the plane, where the pilot was already strapping himself in.
>
> I helped him with his shoulder harness, then jumped out of the cockpit, slammed the belly hatch shut and ran to the wheel well, yelling 'Contact!' as I gave her a shot of prime.
>
> Then I ran to the other wheel well where the prop was

already turning over and gave it a shot of prime. The Hercules coughed, and then roared to life like they always did.

My pilot started taxiing out and I ran for my life to get clear of the airplane before I got run over. As he went by, I noticed the R/O had not closed his rear belly hatch, but there was nothing I could do as he lifted off into the dark sky.

Henderson, who must have eventually noticed and closed his escape hatch, warmed up the radar while Jeffrey responded to the GCI vectors they were getting on the radio.

As I went wheels up, GCI gave me a heading to steer to intercept a 'bogey' which was already being chased by an RAF fighter. The 'bogey' was reported to be low, so I stayed down too. However, the RAF guy was just about out of gas and would have to break off soon.

GCI also informed me that the 'bogey' was probably a recce [reconnaissance] bird, trying to find a convoy and notify another strike group to hit the convoy once he found it.

Bill picked up contact and vectored me in close. Positive visual identification was required at all times and the best way to do that was to get below the unknown and see his profile against the lighter sky above, even if it was at night. This guy was so low, I couldn't get under him because the turbulence from his prop wash would have thrown me into the drink. I had to just hang on and wait.

He began taking violent evasive action, turning quickly right and then left. Bill's job was to keep his head glued to the radar screen and shout 'Left! Right! Left! Right!' and guide me so we could cut the corners and keep up with 'bogey'.

This went on for a while and I told Bill just to hang on. That if this guy was going to do anything, he'd have to climb to do it and when he did so, I would have him at minimum range of about 150 feet.

We hung on his tail for about thirty minutes. Then he started to climb. I was still at 50 feet and all at once he filled my gunsight. I made a quick ID that he was a twin-engined Ju 88, opened fire and immediately noticed my HE rounds hit on his wing and fuselage. The aircraft peeled over to the right and we lost radar contact. GCI also lost the contact.

I could only claim a probable, since I never actually saw him crashing, however, the Intelligence Service confirmed that he never made it back to his base.

Jeffrey won the US DFC for his busy month, both his and the squadron's first. Many months later, the British also recognized Jeffrey's accomplishments by awarding him their DFC as well. Henderson, as was often the case for R/Os, received nothing. Jeffrey today still considers that unfair to his outstanding combat partner.

As April bloomed, numerous personnel changes occurred. Flight Officer Jeffrey was awarded a battlefield commission to second lieutenant, Bill Roble, the last of the enlisted R/Os was promoted to flight officer; and another crew was sent to help out the 416th NFS – pilot Lieutenant Walt Groom and R/O Harold Roth flew into Naples where they promptly scored a kill against a Ju 88 on 9 April. Unfortunately for the 417th, since their crew was on duty with another squadron, they could not claim the victory for their scoreboard. Still, it was nice to know that one of their own hit the enemy.

Other men went home to be instructors in many of the training bases back in America that were churning out replacements for combat squadrons. One of these replacements, personnel specialist Thomas Luke, joined the 417th. He would eventually replace the first sergeant, 'Doc' Hockman, when the squadron moved into Germany. For now, he took a roundabout way to the squadron.

He left the United States on a troopship, unloading at a replacement unit ('repo depot' as it was known) in a French monastery in Algiers. He sat there for several weeks awaiting orders to a unit. These finally came down from above and he crossed the Mediterranean to join the 417th's ground echelon in Corsica. He recalls disembarking from a landing ship tank (LST) a large, flat-bottomed ship that could ground itself on a beach and disgorge its cargo directly onto shore. He was carrying his overcoat, barracks bag, gas mask carrier, and an M1 carbine and had to hump all that gear more than a mile through ankle-deep sand before he could set it down. He thumbed a ride on a truck across the island and found part of the 417th in Borgo.

Back at La Senia, the rest of the squadron stood down in late April, preparing to move, finally, to Corsica. Commanding officer Joe Ehlinger threw a party in celebration of the squadron's accomplishments in Africa and as a way to let off steam before moving up.

Personnel changes happened at La Senia as well. 'Doc' Katzberg diagnosed one of the cooks, Corporal Ernest Griffith with testicular cancer and sent him to hospital to be shipped home for treatment. He unfortunately died shortly thereafter. The challenge of flying the temperamental Beaufighters also became too much for one of the pilots, Second Lieutenant Sam Hooten. He requested and received a transfer to a P-47 single engined day-fighter unit where he had a successful operational tour. Obviously, night fighters were a different breed.

Pilot Ken Nelson went home with his R/O; men from the radar, armaments, radio and engine shops were also sent back to teach others in their specialities. They were replaced with rookies who had to be brought up to speed about life in the 417th.

When the craft and crews arrived at Borgo on 25 April, the squadron was united for the first time in four months. As the senior officer on the base, Ehlinger also assumed the duties of base commander in addition to his flying duties. Operations were resumed on the 29th and they soon found themselves in a protracted struggle to eliminate a potentially dangerous foe nicknamed 'Bedcheck Charlie'. This was a German reconnaissance plane that flew an almost nightly sortie down the length of Corsica, intent on both reconnoitring the build-up of Allied aircraft on the island and demoralizing them by depriving them of precious sleep.

Sometimes a bomb or two was dropped, sometimes an area was sprayed with machine-gun fire, but just his presence was enough to trigger the air-raid warning and send men running to bomb shelters, thus disrupting both operations and sleep patterns.

During May, almost every crew had a go at 'Charlie'; some came tantalizingly close to hitting him but they never destroyed him. So regular were his visits that the crews put up a 'kitty' of $5.00 every time somebody made contact but did not shoot him down. Whichever crew that did nail him would win the prize.

Lieutenant Jack Kirwan and Flight Officer Joe Van Laecken, the crew who drew first blood for the squadron in North Africa, also had the first crack at 'Charlie'. They brought the intercept to a visual and identified it as another Ju 88. Kirwan pumped it full of holes but did not knock it down. He and Van Laecken paid up their $5.00 penalty.

Next to try, on 9 May, was Captain Clarence R. 'Dick' McCray with Flight Officer Robert Hamilton. Hamilton picked up 'Charlie' on his radar and guided McCray to a visual. McCray managed to knock a piece off the plane but they still had to contribute their $5.00 to the kitty when it escaped again.

McCray and Hamilton soon avenged their financial loss, but not against 'Charlie'. Three nights later, they scrambled against a German bombing raid against another airfield on Corsica. They intercepted and shot down a Heinkel He 177 and damaged another during a long sortie against the raid. The 177 was a four-engined bomber, unique in that two engines were geared together on each side to drive one propeller. McCray's combat report reads:

While on Southern Patrol, morning of May 13, 1944, 'TOOTHPASTE' control station advised us that plot [radar contact on the controller's screen] was believed friendly, so we investigated with caution. Obtained AI contact at 0200 hours and followed it in from 4 miles range. Visual was obtained at 1,500 and at a range of 1,000, tentatively identified 'bogey' as a Wellington bomber [an RAF twin-engined medium bomber], influenced by controller's statement that it was believed friendly.

Spent four minutes in very vulnerable position during which time the 'bogey' showed no IFF [identification friend or foe – an electronic 'black box' that gave off an 'I'm friendly' signal). At about 500 range, identified bogey as He-177. We pulled up, speed approx. 220, E/As [enemy aircraft's] 210-220, and opened fire, receiving approx. four bursts of return fire from the tail position, inflicting damage in our a/c's starboard wing and port stabilizers.

We fired two more bursts of 2-3 seconds each. Then the enemy a/c, in three successive peel-offs reduced altitude from 8,000 to 300. After E/A's first peel-off, our a/c got in a 2-3 second burst and observed hits on E/A's vertical fin. At the bottom of the E/A's peel-off, he pulled up sharply, then went into a diving turn, escaping our AI coverage. AI contact not regained.

'TOOTHPASTE' then put us back up to angels 7 [angel was code for 1,000ft – angels 7 – 7,000ft.] and at about 0235, vectored us onto a 'bogey'. At 0245, obtained AI contact and closed in to about 1500 and obtained a visual. Our speed was 220 and the E/A's was 210-220. Gunsight was U/S [unserviceable], so we fired by approximation. The enemy a/c was flying directly into the moon and was very hard to spot. As we closed to about 1,200, E/A dropped small quantity of 'Window'.

Identified E/A as He-177 and closed to about 200 yards. First two second burst gave no visible results and E/A commenced evasive action, consisting of medium and hard turns.

Second burst of three seconds, then cannons stopped. Observed number of 20mm strikes on E/A's starboard nacelle. Flames showed which persisted for five seconds then died out. Continued firing using only .303s, in several 2-3 second bursts until ammo expended. Our windscreen covered by oily mixture. E/A's speed dropped to 135mph and evasive action ceased, apparently due to loss of starboard engines. Action terminated 35-40 miles southeast of Borgo and E/A was losing altitude at such a rate that he could not reach territory friendly to him, let alone make a landing. There was no return fire from the second E/A at any time.

Claim made for and verified as one He-177 probably destroyed and one He-177 damaged by Capt. C.R. McCray and FO R.D. Hamilton.

One of the Heinkels jettisoned his bomb load short of the intended target, a B-25 field south of Borgo, but his bombs struck the south end of the 417th's runway.

'Charlie' showed up the next night and this time it was Captain John Lee, pilot and his R/O, Flight Officer Leonard Potter, who took up the challenge. Following the almost scripted mission, Potter guided his pilot until he could see 'Charlie'. Lee hammered the target severely, making several successful firing passes until the tired Beaufighter let the crew down. Flogged too hard, it simply broke and leaked hydraulic fluid everywhere. The landing gear dropped down forlornly, with no pressure to hold it in the retracted position. The drag from the gear caused such a speed loss that the wounded 'Charlie' was able to escape again.

'Jeff' Jeffrey and Bill Henderson also had a go. Jeffrey says:

He was a recce bird out looking for convoys and giving Corsica the once over as well during his flight. I think everybody in the squadron had a go at him. He generally escaped us by flying so low that it was impossible for anyone to get a shot off at him.

Our planes could not shoot downward, and when you are after somebody flying low, it is not wise to try to dive at him shooting, then hope to pull up just after passing him at 50-100ft altitude, particularly when doing better than 200 knots! I chased him many times but one night in mid-May stands out.

It was around midnight and GCI vectored us after a 'bogey'. Bill got radar contact at the maximum range of about 6 miles and the chase was on. In the dark of night, you couldn't see the enemy except at very close ranges so you depended on your R/O for flight directions.

Charlie was doing very violent evasive action but Bill hung on tight to him, shouting directions for me to fly. 'Right! Right! Left! Left! Climb! Descend!' I listened to Bill and my hands instinctively moved the controls, following his instructions. We moved into minimum range of about 150ft, 100ft above the cold waters of the Med. Any closer to the 'bogey' and the radar couldn't display the blip since the ground returns were so strong that close to the deck and still I couldn't see him.

Bill kept hollering for me to 'Go down! Go down!' By this time, I'm at 50ft and getting bounced around from the propwash of the 'bogey', looking out like mad for a visual on the guy and trying not to turn my airplane into a submarine all at the same time. Bill, glued to his scope and concentrating on the target's movements, was not aware of our flying predicament. He kept calling out 'Low and dead ahead!'

In the excitement of the chase and tuned in to Bill's voice in the combat situation, I must have nudged the yoke forward without realizing it because when I snuck a quick look at my instruments, the radar altimeter was reading zero feet and about to turn itself into a depth gauge.

Forgetting the target for a moment and expecting to see fish outside my canopy at any second, I thought, 'Well, this is it!'

Ever so gently, I eased the yoke back, hoping to regain some precious altitude. It was like driving your car when a wheel eases off the side of the road. You don't want to yank the steering wheel for fear of losing control, so you have to ever so gently ease the wheel back on the pavement.

All at once I felt a jolt, heard a 'whump' and lost a few knots of airspeed and the engines started vibrating so much that I could barely read the instruments. However, I was gaining altitude, but ever so slowly.

Bill, still head down in the back, keyed the intercom to ask me what happened. My heart was beating so hard that I couldn't even answer him. Next, the GCI station radioed me to ask why I was breaking off the intercept!

All I could croak out in reply was 'Pigeons to home plate [course for home base]!' and that I had hit the water and the airplane was vibrating badly.

After we did make it back, we inspected the aircraft and found both props bent from striking the water. That was what made the engines vibrate so much. Also, the underside of the fuselage below the horizontal stabilizers was damaged from hitting the water's surface.

We had been extremely lucky. The radar altimeter had an error factor of plus or minus 10ft. We must have been on the plus side, but not by much.

So Charlie got away again and another $5.00 went towards the kitty.

The squadron suffered a stunning loss on 25 May but not through combat. One of the cooks, Sergeant Harry Tucker was killed and five other cooks riding with him were badly injured in a vehicle accident. Driving in a weapons carrier (a type of truck), the men missed a curve and tumbled down an embankment. It was quite a blow for that many men to be lost at one time.

At the end of the month, John Kirwan and Joe Van Laecken scrambled after another 'bogey'. The policy of visually identifying every intercepted aircraft paid off this time. After a twenty-minute chase, they flew close enough to identify it as an American B-25 and held their fire. The B-25's tail gunner, however, did not and hosed tracers at the Beaufighter. Kirwan peeled off before he was hit and returned safely to Borgo. The next day, the squadron intelligence section reported that a B-25 claimed it had shot down a German Ju 88 and had even seen one crewman bale out!

CHAPTER 7

The old saw about combat being 'five minutes of terror mixed with hours and hours of boredom' applied to the 417th NFS as much as it did to any unit. Most of the flying patrols did not come into contact with the enemy. Even when GCI picked up a radar contact, it often faded before the 417th could respond.

When not flying, the officers and men endured relatively primitive living conditions – 'relatively' in that to an infantryman carrying a rifle in the mud of Italy, the 417th's accommodation would have seemed posh, but compared to today's standard of living, they were really roughing it.

They lived in tents, ate outside or in tents, and worked on the aircraft either outside in the weather or in workshops set up in tents. Their latrines or 'privies' were crude wooden multi-hole affairs over large pits, with the view open to all passing by. They bathed in open-air showers made from Lister bags hung from a post or a tree. Some of the more creatively minded built heated showers constructed from 55-gallon drums filled with water heated via salvaged piping that ran through a heater using highly flammable 100 octane aircraft fuel.

Radar technician Carroll Poole described the radar shop being set up in a tarpaper and scrap-timber shack. During the spring and summer months, it was pretty effective, if a bit hot to work in amid the vacuum tubes and soldering irons that were some of the tools of the early electronics trade. Later, once the squadron moved to France and the bitter cold, they heated it by burning 100 octane fuel in a cut-away barrel. They set up a drum of fuel outside, and piped the volatile brew through copper tubing that fed the open drum. The contraption made the radar shop nice and warm but kept them on their toes to keep it from erupting in flames.

Their method of cleaning out the soot build-up in the stovepipe venting the exhaust was also ingenious – and equally dangerous. The pipe was built from the cylindrical containers used to ship signalling flares. When soot deposits built up, they simply unhooked one end of the pipe, jammed a flare pistol into the end and pulled the trigger. The flare projectile rushing through the piping scoured it clean as a whistle. It must have made for quite a show as well, with copious amounts of smoke and pyrotechnics.

Once the squadron was back together, the quality of food improved as the cooks put on meals of dehydrated potatoes, spam, dehydrated eggs, and occasionally fresh meat from events like a pig roast. The near-daily bread baking by the cooks was appreciated by the rest of the squadron. Several Yugoslav prisoners of war were assigned as mess helpers. These men, grateful to be out of combat on behalf of the Germans, did their duties cheerfully. Their wild gesticulations and strange language provided hours of amusement for the men as they lined up for their food.

On Corsica, the squadron's tents were about ¼ mile from the flight line. Up in the hills a river served as a bathing and swimming spot. Near to that was a spring heated by geothermal energy that several men diverted into the river to make for nice heated baths.

The squadron's medical officer, the newly promoted flight surgeon Captain Arthur Katzberg says that as a rule, the men were young, mostly eighteen to twenty-one, and healthy. He and his team rarely had need for a sick call for colds, flu and the like. Instead, one of his primary duties was to ensure that venereal disease was diagnosed and treated. This malady, a bane for armies for centuries past, affected the US forces as much as any others. Army Air Forces headquarters put out guidance that all personnel had to be checked monthly. 'Doc' Katzberg and the squadron first sergeant, 'Doc' Hockman, made surprise 2 a.m. checks.

They would enter a tent where six to eight men were sleeping, rouse them and have them drop their trousers for what was known as a 'short arm inspection'. There was no disciplinary punishment meted out for having the disease, but many men who frequented brothels did not report for treatment when they thought they might have something because in this era before widespread, convenient antibiotics, the treatment was painful and involved inserting a caustic concoction of medicine up the urethra. Many are the men who believed the cure was worse than the disease!

'Doc' Katzberg's contribution to the squadron was more than just healing the body, however. Besides the intimate inspections, Katzberg performed a role as psychiatrist as well. He would meet the men after they landed from their missions, and besides issuing the medicinal booze that could calm twitchy nerves stretched by hours of tense flying in dark and often stormy weather, perhaps being shot at, perhaps enduring crashing or baling out, he would watch for those who showed signs of unusual stress. He would talk to them, letting them pour out their anxieties, and usually just the opportunity to voice the long-bottled-up fears was enough. In the macho world of a combat squadron, it was not manly to talk about being scared, so the fear just built up inside a man. By offering a friendly ear, 'Doc' could let that pressure escape for a while.

The pilots and R/Os knew that he understood what they were going through because he often flew missions himself. By jury-rigging a seat behind the pilot, he would go along on operational sorties and watch both the crew and the action during the mission. Crouched on top of the ammunition cases for the four 20mms, with a lap belt holding him down while the Beaufighter lurched around the sky, Katzberg experienced the same moments of terror as the flying crews. He was there on several missions when the Germans shot back. He recalled seeing the tracer fire go by the front cockpit windows and instinctively ducking to avoid the bullets, sheepishly pulling himself upright afterwards as the glowing orange-yellow fireballs flicked away at the last minute. He flew twenty combat missions during his time with the squadron and earned the Air Medal for his airborne efforts.

For more severe cases of combat fatigue, he would take a man off flying for a few days to let his nerves simmer down and that worked wonders as well. Only in a few cases did a flyer not recover his courage enough to continue combat flying. For those unfortunate few, Katzberg had no choice but to recommend that the individual be removed from flying. When that happened, the man was gone almost overnight. It was bad for morale for those still in the game to have someone who could not take it any more hanging around. The British called such a condition LMF (lack of moral fibre) and whisked the poor man away instantly. The US Army followed the same practice, which was necessary to keep a fighting unit fighting.

'Doc' Katzberg also showed some shrewd bargaining skills when the unit moved to Corsica. By exchanging some issue whisky for wood and tarpaper from an Army construction battalion, he acquired enough for the 417th to build a really nice enlisted dayroom and bar. In there, the men had the opportunity to play dice, poker, draughts and chess, and write in comparative luxury compared with their canvas tents.

One area where he could not provide much help was getting replacement parts for the aircraft. Even something as basic but critical as tyres required hours and hours of searching to find. When they could be found, they were only good for a couple of take-offs and landings before they had to be replaced. Britain, under severe shortages of critical war material like rubber, ordered its aircraft manufacturers to use the thinnest, most economical tyres possible for their designs. Bristol, the Beau's producer, used thin, slick, non-treaded tyres. This design worked satisfactorily on the smooth concrete or grass runways and taxiways of an English aerodrome, but in the harsh, tactical conditions of a forward airfield like Borgo, it could not take the punishment. The dirt and rocks that were Borgo's runway and the steel planking of the hard stands shredded the tyres, making them unusable after only a few flights. So thin was the rubber that the tyres had to be covered between flights because the oil dripping from the Beau's Hercules engines would eat through them in just a couple of days.

One solution to the tyre shortage was to send the B-25, the 'Strawberry Roan', to airfields and supply dumps around the Mediterranean. Then the squadron's crew chiefs and pilots would beg, borrow and steal enough tyres to get the unit through a few more days. They found a cache of precious tyres in a rubbish dump outside Algiers and crammed the B-25's bomb bay with three sets of wheels. These trips also served as a way to send a couple of men away from the camp and get some much needed rest and relaxation in the various locations visited by the 'Roan'.

The 417th had several baseball teams during its life, for both internal and inter-unit competition. Most of the squadron maintenance shops fielded a team to play in local competitions. The best from each of the internal teams banded together to represent the night fighters against the other units. They did quite well and the games are always a topic of discussion at the 417th's reunions.

The talented men of the squadron put out their own newspaper, *Grounded*. It featured tall tales and embarrassing anecdotes about various characters in the squadron. Regular issues of newspapers and books from the Red Cross fulfilled the need for the hard news, as did the Army's own *Stars and Stripes*.

Occasionally they put on talent shows, and films shown outdoors completed the official entertainment. But drinking was probably the most popular pastime. Most men drew a beer ration once or twice a month and as the photographs show, these bottles were pretty large. Whenever squadron aircraft diverted to more populated areas like Naples, they would come back stuffed to the gills with whatever bottles could be found.

Demon rum sometimes led to punishment for some infraction. Transgressions like oversleeping and being late for duty, late returning from a pass or the like were dealt with 'in-house'. The commander, in consultation with the first sergeant, meted out punishment as the situation warranted. If it was a man's first offence and he had a good reputation for solid work, then he might only receive some hours on KP, peeling potatoes or emptying bins. If it was more serious like being drunk on duty or it was not the first offence, then the man could be demoted, 'taking a stripe' as it was called. Besides the humiliation of losing rank, it affected a man's wallet because he also now got the pay of the lower rank.

The squadron diary humorously describes one such event: 'T/Sgts Facciolla and Maupin and Pfc Garmise were appointed corporals this date per squadron orders.' It was a neat way of playing up the private's good fortune and including the demotion of the two unfortunates in the same sentence.

'Sleepy' Hissett, in an interview sixty years later commented that he started out in the service as a private and was 'busted' a couple of times, leaving the service only one rank higher. It seems it had something to do with drink, Naples, and a B-25 taking off on 5 June, 1944 without the proper code of the day and not scheduled as a mission. The 417th's B-25 showed up as a 'bogey' on radar warning sites along the Mediterranean. Intercepted by North American P-51 Mustangs, the B-25 was identified and the unauthorized flight reported. Naturally, the 417th's commanding officer was given a dressing down for allowing such an operation and it has been a maxim of military services since time immemorial that 'shit rolls downhill'. Upon arriving back at Corsica, every man in the B-25 was given a summary court martial and 'busted' at least one rank – all for a drink. Still, Hissett says today, it was worth it.

Unfortunately, besides the standard hangovers and headaches from over-imbibing, one young man, late in the war, made a deadly mistake in reaching for a bottle beside his cot. Private R.S. Melancon, engine mechanic, instead of taking a swig of scotch swallowed a large dose of carbon tetrachloride cleaning solution. This mix, used to clean build up on the Beaufighter's spark plugs and magnetos, poisoned him and he died within hours.

Although the squadron did not have its own chaplain, the Army Air Forces did send one regularly to the unit for spiritual guidance. He would hold open-air services which were usually well attended.

During the early summer of 1944, many more personnel rotated home. Especially among the aircrew, the constant stress of combat and the potential for combat in ragged aeroplanes wore the men out. After flying the required number of combat hours, they went home, usually as instructors in the night-fighter school, to pass on their hard-won knowledge to the next generation of crews. For example, R/O Second Lieutenant Joe Van Laecken completed his overseas tour with 218.5 combat hours out of his total flying hours of 366. He flew more than 125 combat missions during his tour of operations. He was especially glad to be going home for it would be the first time he would see his daughter, who was born in September 1942.

Chief among the other lucky ones going home was Major Joe

Ehlinger. He left on 16 June, and was replaced by Captain Bill Larson, the operations officer. Larson's place was taken by Captain Dick McCray. Some of the replacements coming in included Lieutenant Harold Heinecke, R/O, and his pilot, Lieutenant Tom Hill. Russ Gaebler and Everett Packham, pilot and R/O, also arrived along with Second Lieutenant Robert Inglis, pilot, and replacement Flight Officer Ted Hearne, R/O. They took up their posts on 5 July. Heinecke should have joined the squadron several months earlier but in his travel to the unit, he snapped an ankle on one of Oran's cobblestoned streets. The fact that the accident occurred on New Year's Eve was probably purely coincidental. As various crews finished their tours, this constant rotation of personnel would become a squadron fixture, with old heads going home and new men taking their places. They quickly oriented themselves to the pace of life in a combat squadron.

CHAPTER 8

On 3 July, Captain Herm Stirnus had a crack at 'Bedcheck Charlie'. What was different on this sortie was that although Stirnus and his R/O were still in a worn out old Beaufighter, it did have the latest radar, the Mk VIII (US SCR-720), which had a much better low-level capability. It could filter out most of the clutter from ground returns, leaving a much 'cleaner' picture for the R/O to work from. Also flying with Stirnus was flight surgeon 'Doc' Katzberg. On this mission, he watched a man in the ultimate of frustrating situations. According to the 417th's operational diary:

> Capt H.A. Stirnus had a tough break. After a hard chase, he had closed to 100ft on a Jerry. Had him lined up in his sights for a perfect shot, pressed the button and not a single gun fired. Causes for gun failure could not be determined as they functioned properly later.

However, that was not the whole story. 'Doc' Katzberg crouched on his makeshift seat on the ammunition boxes of the four 20mm cannons when the crew intercepted the Ju 88, again, scooting along at extremely low level. Stirnus did a good job of closing in, but when he squeezed the tit, absolutely nothing happened. Almost crying in frustration, Stirnus broke off the engagement and turned for home. Katzberg, however, knew that with the latest lot of Beaufighters the squadron was getting, the gun switches were different. On previous models, there was a button to fire the 20mm cannons and another to fire the .303 machine-guns. To fire both, the pilot had to toggle both switches. In this latest variant, however, the switches were wired into only one button. In other words, if the pilot squeezed the right trigger, all ten weapons would blast forth. Squeezing the other switch did absolutely nothing. Stirnus had simply hit the wrong switch. Doc Katzberg pointed this new feature out to Stirnus, who pulled the correct trigger and the Beaufighter shuddered under the recoil of everything erupting. What was particularly galling for Stirnus was that this was his last combat mission. He would head for the Zone of the Interior (ZI) as military called the USA in another five days. So not only did his 'finger trouble' cost him his only victory of the war, but he had to pay up his $5.00 toward the kitty.

Two nights later after Stirnus's experience, a new crew consisting of Lieutenant Wilson and Flight Officer Berry took off on a patrol, easing into the operational schedule. About twenty minutes after take-off, the right engine exploded. Radioing a mayday, and unable to maintain altitude and too far from Corsica to make it back in time, they ditched into calm seas. Wilson did a good job bringing the crippled plane down and both crew members were aboard an air-sea rescue amphibian within minutes of hitting the water. They flew another patrol the next night.

On 8 July, new men Hill and Heinecke shot a piece off 'Charlie'. Heinecke says of the combat:

> We did get credit for a 'probable' when we were flying out of Corsica. We were vectored onto a Ju 188 [a variant of the Ju 88 with longer wings] that was flying about 3,000 – 4,000ft. I'll have to confess that I can't take much credit for that 'victory' because we had been at a higher altitude and I had all I could do to pick out the blip made by the Ju because of the sea returns on the radar [They were flying with a Mk IV radar]. Anyhow, the rear gunner on the Ju 188 started shooting at us before we opened fire at him. Hill saw some of our shots hit and the Ju 188 dove away from us. We were given credit for a 'probable' because the GCI radar lost contact with him. Before the engagement he had two blips on his scope, afterwards he only had one and we were still flying.

> After we got on the ground, we went over the Beau with a fine-tooth comb but couldn't find a single bullet hole, but the way those tracers were flying past my canopy, I couldn't believe it.

Even high-ranking visitors from the United States had a go at 'Charlie'. Several nights after Heinecke's adventure, Colonel Winston Kratz, the commander of night-fighter training in California, visited the operational units to see how he could improve the training for his students. A very experienced pilot, he flew a sortie starting at dusk on 16 July. GCI vectored him onto a contact at extremely long range, but after an exhausting chase he was unable to close for a visual. The 'bogey' got away and Kratz gave his $5.00 to the squadron.

Finally, after dozens of chases, the 417th nailed 'Bedcheck Charlie'. A new crew, Inglis and Hearne, on only their fourth operational mission, were given vectors by GCI to a 'bogey' skirting Corsica. Hearne obtained radar contact and brought Inglis close enough to identify a Ju 88 down low. Inglis brought his Beau in close and opened fire.

Over the radio, he reported that he had seen the enemy crash into the water and was going down to take a closer look. No further word was heard from them and they never landed back at Borgo. A search at daybreak revealed debris and survival dinghies from both aircraft at the crash site, but no survivors. The kitty, grown now to a fair size, paid for a bittersweet party for the squadron.

Towards the end of July, the squadron switched from a primarily defensive role in patrolling and defending against *Luftwaffe* incursions to an offensive one by taking the fight over German-held territory, flying intruder patrols to seek out both enemy aircraft and ground targets. Now the Germans, already under pressure from the advancing Allied armies and air forces in the west of France since the D-Day invasions, would get no respite in the south either. The squadron was ordered to fly two to four patrols per night, disrupting the flow of German ground transport whenever they saw it.

These intruder missions sought out trains, trucks and airfields intending to destroy as much German war material and the means to move it as they could. The 417th and other US night-fighter squadrons, destroyed hundreds of trucks and dozens of trains during the course of the war. These missions were dangerous; attacking heavily defended ground targets at night was no walk in the park. Yet the percentage of aircraft and crews

e 417th Night Fighter Squadron takes shape, Kissimmee, Florida, March 1943. *(417th NFS)*

uglas P-70 Night Fighter, used as a training aircraft by the US Beaufighter and Black low squadrons. *(NARA)*

Original 417th NFS squadron atch. *(417th NFS)*

What the well dressed aircrew wears ship out. F/O Rayford W. 'Jeff' Jeffrey (L), pilot, and Lt Carleton B. Frazee, weather officer at Camp Kilmer prior shipping to England. Note web gear with canteens, etc. (Jeff

RMS *Queen Elizabeth* in post-war paint work. Entire Army divisions could and were transported by this one gigantic ship. (NA

Wartime snapshot looking over a Beaufighter pilot's head. Note the outstanding visibility due to the large cockpit windows. (Au

Wartime photo from R/O's position looking forward toward the cockpit. *(Alan Wallis)*

Beaufighter pilot's 'office.' *(NationalMuseum of the USAF)*

w to the left (port) of a Merlin-engined Beaufighter Mk. II. thor)

SS *Durban Castle*, the 417th's transport from England to North Africa. *(417th N*

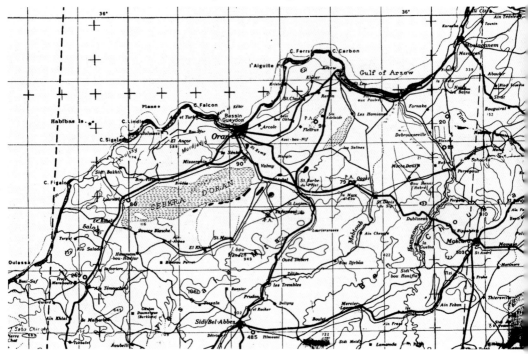

Chart of the 417th's main African operating areas. *(417th N*

Tent living areas, 417th NFS at Tafaroui, Algeria, North Africa, 1943. *(417th*

Squadron roll-call formation, possibly at Tafaroui, 1943. *(417th NFS)*

Next to the flightline, the chow hall was probably one of the most important squadron areas. Here is the squadron's deluxe accommodation in North Africa.

(417th NFS)

Tafaroui movie theatre. *(417th NFS)*

Maintenance chief M Sgt Earl Weatherald in jeep passenger's seat with native North Africans, 1943.
(417th N)

Sgt Charlie Farbach in Arab taxi, Oran, 1943. *(417th NFS)*

Engineering shop members Tatum and Gathright perched on the port Hercules engine. They had to spend many hours working on these oily, complicated moto *(417th NFS)*

Hank Englehardt, crew chief, in front of a 417th Beaufighter. Visible is the tyre cover to protect the thin rubber from dripping oil. *(417th NFS)*

MK VI Beaufighter equipped with the MK IV AI radar, note the difference in the nose line and antenna as compared to the later MK VIII radar. This is actually a 416th NFS bird Italy. *(NARA)*

417th aircraft returning to Tafaroui from a night flying test, prior to launching on operational missions after nightfall. *(NARA)*

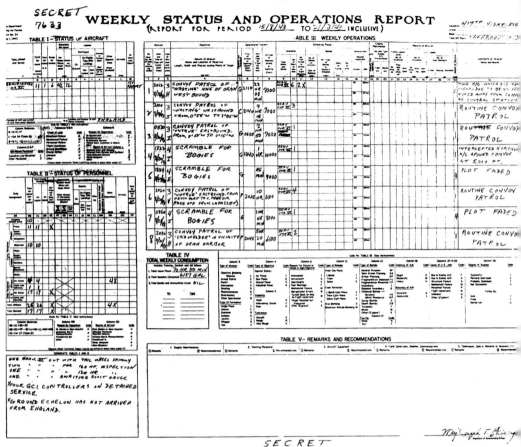

Squadron operation report for the period 15-21 August 1943.

(417th N)

Refueling the squadron's Hawker Hurricane, LB595. The Hurricane served valiantly dur[ing] the early part of the war, particularly during the Battle of Britain. By 1943, fighter technolo[o]gy had largely passed it by and it was obsolescent and relegated to other duties like grou[nd] attack. This aircraft served as a 'hack,' letting the pilots practise flying without taking an op[er] ational aircraft out of service.

(417th N)

rl 'Sleepy' Hissett
tside the cockpit of
s' Beaufighter. As a
w chief, he was
sponsible for the air-
ift being ready to fly.
crew chief 'owned'
e aircraft, the aircrew
it borrowed it.

(417th NFS)

all too familiar sight on a wartime airfield. Here ground crew observe the fire and
oke from a crashed fighter. In this case, it was a Free French P-39 and not one of their
n Beaufighters.

(NARA)

Rare in-flight Beaufighter photo. This image was captured during the squadron's move to Corsica.

(417th NFS)

Junker Ju 88, the Luftwaffe's 'jack of all trades.' Used effectively as a medium bomber, night-fighter and reconnaissance aircraft, it was one of the most often faced threats of the 417th.

(NARA)

arl Hissett lounges against another crew
hief's Beaufighter. This one decorated with a
ugs Bunny' character clutching a fur-
ugh pass. *(417th NFS)*

Heading out for a hop; what the well
dressed USAAF night-fighter crew wore.
(417th NFS)

riginal squadron aircrews, Tafaroui, North Africa. Many of them never came home.
(417th NFS)

417th NFS, Oran, No. Africa 1943/44

Graphic depiction of the mud at Tafaroui, November 1943. *(417th NFS)*

417th flightline, Tafaroui, September 1943. *(NARA)*

417th baseball team in North Africa. *(417th NI*

The 'Kissimmee Cowgirl' Beaufighter, a reminder of the squadron's origins back in Florida. *(417th NFS)*

Map of Corsica during the 417th's stay. *(417th NFS)*

The North American B-25 'Mitchell' bomber that the 417th used as a hack and as a transport, the *'Strawberry Roan.'* *(417th NFS)*

En route to Corsica.

(417th NFS)

Sgt. Paul Peyron, flight engineer for the *Strawberry Roan'* at work
(417th NFS)

Slit trench in Corsica like the one Major Joe Ehlinger was tossed out of during a bombing attack.
(417th NFS)

E. 'Tom' Luke, sums up his feelings for his foxhole accommodations in Corsica.
(417th NFS)

Privacy is just another casualty of war. Here men of the 417th answer the call of nature. *(417th NFS)*

Squadron headquarters at Borgo Airfield, Corsica, April 1944.

(417th NF

Swimming hole on a river several miles from the airfield.

(417th N

...ayroom in Corsica. Many of the materials used to build the building came from some ...vvy trading by flight surgeon, Dr. Arthur Katzberg. *(417th NFS)*

...ative Corsicans with squadron personnel. *(417th NFS)*

...e Mediterranean was also available for relaxation during time off. *(417th NFS)*

Worship service on Corsica. (417th NI

Jeffery's plane after crash-landing following combat on March 28, 1944. Jeffrey downed a
Ju 88 but was hit in return in the foot. Also, Jeffrey's hydraulics were shot out, so he was
unable to lower the gear. Both Jeffrey and R/O Bill Henderson walked away from this on
This was the second of two kills Jeffrey scored in this Beaufighter. (Jeffr

Heinkel He 177 Luftwaffe heavy bomber. This aircraft coupled two engines to each propeller.
Not particularly well-like by its crews, it had a fatal tendency to leak gasoline onto the
engine manifolds when manoeuvring. The results were usually catastrophic. (NAI

Moving day - LSTs (landing ship tank) on the Corsican beach to on-load the 417th and other cargo.

417th map of Mediterranean operations.

Medals presentation: from left to right, Brig Gen Craigie, 1st Lt Rayford W. Jeffrey, Capt Bill Carson, Capt McCray.

Arriving at the harbour of St Raphael, France, September 1944. (417th N

The airfield at Le Vallon, France. Visible are the Beaufighters of the 415th and 417th NFS, as well as several other aircraft types. (NAR

The Le Vallon control tower, 1944. (417th N

Construction on 417th hanger before calamity struck. *(417th NFS)*

The hangar after 'Le Mistral' wind came to visit. *(417th NFS)*

Officers' country at Le Vallon. Notice the thick fir trees used as windbreaks, October 1944. *(417th NFS)*

Enlisted tents during the frigid 1944-45 winter at Le Vallon. *(417th NF*

Maintenance facilities at Le Vallon. *(417th NF*

Typical heavy snowfall at Le Vallon. *(417th NF*

how hall at Le Vellon. *(417th NFS)*

Medic Nick Rapauano at squadron aid
station. *(417th NFS)*

eaning mess kits after a meal. *(417th NFS)*

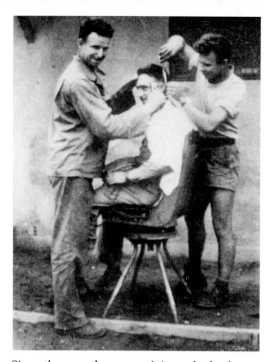

Same for laundry service. *(417th NI*

Since the squadron wasn't issued a barber,
they had to make do. *(417th NFS)*

The intense cold at Le Vallon required a constant replenishment of each tent stove's wood
supply. Here a work detail cuts up logs, a far cry from the technical specialties of most of
the men. *(417th N*

ermath of the tent fire in February, 1945. A little excitement goes a long way to judge by
crowd. *(417th NFS)*

'ilot Morris 'Dirty' Dalton goes for a
anteen refill run. *(417th NFS)*

esides drinking and flying, there wasn't much to do in a wartime squadron. Here a
roup of pilots and R/Os 'bat the breeze.' *(417th NFS)*

R/O William Work, Morris 'Dirty' Dalton, and unknown passenger pose after a mission. *(Morris Dalton)*

'Woody' Grange at the entrance to his ten You'd never know of his string of harrow ing adventures by looking at his face. *(417th NFS)*

Pilot and operations officer Dick McCray, Le Vallon, France, 1944. *(417th NFS)*

Replacement crew, William Rial, left, and R/O James Chelf. *(417th N*

aufighter crew Bob Condon, left and his
'O, Dick 'Corny' Cornwall.

(417th NFS)

uadron Leader George Parret, RAF GCI
ntroller visited the squadron regularly
iile in France. His visits gave valuable
dback to the crews on how they were
rforming. *(417th NFS)*

Wartime tourists in Avignon, France. From
left to right: Dr. Katzberg, pilots Hienecke
and Deakyne, weather officer Frazee.
(417th NFS)

Tom Luke and Jack Choojian share a drink
and a smoke, Le Vallon, October 1944.
(417th NFS)

Foreground, the second CO of the squadron, Major William Larson sitting on left, line chief M Sgt Earl Weatherald and Capt J.D. Brown, adjutant, with feet on cylinder. (417th NFS)

M Sgt Earl Weatherald outside the Engineering shop, Le Vallon, fall, 1944. (417th N.

From left to right, crew chief L.A. Miller, 1st Sgt Charles 'Doc' Hockman, Paul Peyron, Le Zuckerman. (417th N

cohol was a major entertainment. The officers had better access to liquor while the
listed men mainly had to make do with beer. But with the size of these bottles, a good
uzz' probably wasn't too hard to come by! *(417th NFS)*

pical winter's day at Le Vallon. Note the disparity in uniforms and attire. Almost anything
nt if it kept you warm. *(417th NFS)*

Another way to kill time was squadron sports. The 417th fielded several baseball teams; horseshoes was another popular pastime, as was, weather permitting, volleyball as seen here.

(417th NF

Dr. Marvin Weinberg, classical pianist, radar technician and flight surgeon. *(417th NFS)*

The 417th's Beaufighters were unable to climb high enough to knock down Luftwaffe reconnaissance aircraft over Marseille, so the RAF sent in one of their de Havilland Mosquito night-fighters from 255 Squadron to deal with the threat. *(417th NFS)*

Bob Condon enjoying a well earned smoke after completing a night flying test in
Beaufighter KW274   *(417th NFS)*

Fine profile photo of KW191. The RAF used a serial numbering system consisting
of alphabetic letters and numbers. The US Beaufighter squadrons kept those serial
numbers since the aircraft were only 'borrowed' from the British.   *(417th NFS)*

Aftermath of a blown tyre at take-off, Tafaroui, North Africa, 1943.   *(417th NFS)*

An all too-familiar sight; maintenance crews salvaging a wrecked Beaufighter.
     (417th NFS)

matic series of photos of remains of the October 16, 1944 crash of Lts Howard and
ngone in V8558 at Le Vallon. *(417th NFS)*

Another Beaufighter meets its fate after engine failure during the late fall of 1944 when 2/3 of the squadron's aircraft were destroyed. *(417th N*

Remnants of ND296, lost on landing, Le Vallon, 1944. Pilot Davis was badly burned in t crash, but survived. *(417th N*

The crew walked away from this one without at scratch. *(417th N*

More than three dozen men from the 417th lost their lives while overseas. Here the grave marker of pilot Edward Graybill still lies in the military cemetery at Rhone, France. *(417th NFS)*

Tail on view of Beaufighter V8899. *(417th NFS)*

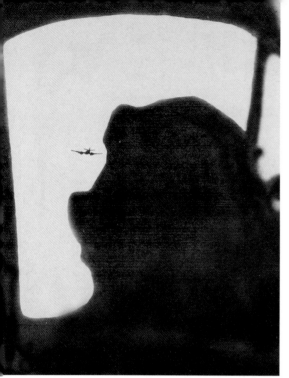

Dusk photo of Beaufighter setting out on patrol. Another Beaufighter can be seen just to the left of the pilot's head.

(Author)

Junkers Ju 290 like the one downed in d matic fashion by Lts Campbell and McCullen on Dec 28, 1944. This one has been caught in daylight by RAF Spitfire off the coast of Sicily. *(NARA)*

2nd Lt Robert McCullen receiving the Distinguished Flying Cross for downing 'Barcel Charlie,' France, 1945.

(417th N

Maintenance officer, 1st Lt Kenneth Campbell (no relation to the pilot with the same last name) congratulates M Sgt Earl Weatherald on being awarded the Legion of Merit LOM) for his early efforts in keeping the worn-out Beaufighters flyable. The fourth highest military decoration at the time, the LOM was rarely awarded to an enlisted man, thus all the more honour to Weatherald and the rest of the squadron's ground crews.

(417th NFS)

A captured Messerschmitt Bf-109 like the one in which 'Duff' Campbell met his fate. *(417th NFS)*

One of the first P-61 'Black Widows' of the 417th, nicknamed '*Rhoddea.*' The pilot sat in the front cockpit, the rarely carried gunner in the one above the pilot and the R/O occupied his station at the rear of the fuselage (not visible in this photo). Note the nose-art so prevalent of the era. *(417th NFS)*

First 417th P-61s at St. Dizier, France, March 1945. *(417th NFS)*

Changing of the guard, the long-serving Beaufighter lined up alongside its replacement, the incomparable Northrop P-61, St. Dizier, France, 1945. *(417th NFS)*

1 cockpit. *(417th NFS)*

R-720 radar scope. For operations in the aircraft, a long tubular hood extended from the
e of the scope so that the R/O could look into it during all conditions. *(417th NFS)*

Ju 88 that intentionally crashed and surrendered at the airfield, St. Dizier, France,
March 1945. *(417th NFS)*

George Aubill, pilot, and R/O Tom Hart in front of their mount, the 'Lonesome Polecat'.   (417th NFS)

m Hart in the R/O's osition at the rear of e 'Widow's' fuselage.
(417th NFS)

End of the *'Lonesome Polecat.'* (417th NFS)

Probably the best night-fighter of any combatant during World War II, the Northrop P-61 'Black Widow.' (NARA)

417th NFS P-61 in Germany equipped with long-range drop tanks. (417th NFS)

...aintenance officer, Capt Kenneth Campbell, sails for home, 1945. Campbell was with the ...uadron from its activation until after the end of the war. *(417th NFS)*

...ich Ziebart sets off for post-war duty with ...e 417th NFS in occupied Germany, 1946.
(Rich Ziebart)

Terry Carter takes a break for a 'photo op,' Germany, 1946. *(417th NFS)*

John Roberson in the cockpit of a P-61, Germany, 1946.   *(417th NFS)*

Rich Ziebart doing his duty as a radar technician, Germany 1946.   *(417th NFS)*

P-61 take off, Kessel, Germany, 1946. *(417th NFS)*

In-flight photo taken from R/O's position in a P-61, over Germany, 1946. *(417th NFS)*

Scrapping surplus P-61s by packing the fuselage with explosives, 1946. *(417th NFS)*

Gutted 'Widows.'   *(417th NFS)*

stroying a beautiful airplane; another P-61 meets an inglorious demise. *(417th NS)*

e second wartime 417th NFS squadron
tch. Compare this one to the original patch
n the first one, a caveman sets off to club
e enemy; fitting to the primitive state of
ght fighting at the beginning of the war. In
s version, a magician, the 'R/O' uses a
stal ball to find bandits and guides the
ot up front flying the broomstick. *(417th
S)*

Capt Dick Larson, the third commander of the
417th and his R/O, Capt Joe Draper. Draper
was also the senior observer for the squadron,
responsible for checking out the new R/Os on
operational flying and intercepts. *(Joe Draper)*

APPROCHING END OF

LANDING ROLL

JUST SCRAMBLED

Unknown artist drew these caricatures to depict common flying hazards faced by the aircrew of the 417th NFS.

DROPPING IT IN

LOW SLOW FINAL

lost was far smaller than in aerial combat.

Veterans Ted Deakyne and Joe Kirwan flew the inaugural intruder sorties, elated at the break in the monotony of endless patrols. Deakyne, as we have seen, had also flown these types of missions while a member of the RCAF flying Mosquitoes. The US aviators flew over the lower Rhône valley in France looking for trouble. They – and succeeding crews – found it, and enjoyed the challenge. Gun positions, radar stations, troop bivouac areas and the railway lines from Cannes to Genoa all found themselves menaced by the night fighters, all in preparation for the coming invasion of southern France on 15 August 1944.

Designed to increase the pressure on the Germans, this second invasion, codenamed Operation Dragoon, poured tens of thousands of troops, tanks and supporting equipment onto the Continent. The squadron's intruder missions as well as their old standard role of harbour protection occupied much of the succeeding months. Eventually, the squadron would be based on the French mainland but for now, it still called Corsica home.

Lieutenant Willie Williamson and his R/O, Lieutenant Dan Cordell, scored the last airborne kill by the 417th before the move into France. Their prey was another 'Bedcheck Charlie' reconnaissance aircraft. On 3 August, GCI sent them after a 'bogey'. Cordell, operating the Mk VIII radar, soon obtained contact and kept up a running commentary to Williamson, guiding him to visual range. At this point, Williamson identified the aircraft as an enemy, another Ju 188. As he crept in, the target changed course, turning and flying up the path created by the moon's reflection against the Mediterranean – perfect for seeing the quarry. Williamson used the bonus light to fly in even closer before unleashing the Beau's formidable weaponry.

The Ju 188's cockpit exploded in a shower of plexiglass shards. Engines flaring briefly, the aircraft exploded, the flaming pieces showering into the Mediterranean. It was a textbook example of what night fighting was supposed to be. 'Jeff' Jeffreys remembers Willie coming back that night to the tent the men shared and being so excited by the combat and victory that he kept Jeffrey up all night telling and retelling the story.

As the fighting from Dragoon moved off the beaches and further inland, the 417th was notified that it would soon be moving up into France as well. They ceased operation at Borgo in early September, packed everything into crates, and drove to the beaches of eastern Corsica where their lift to the mainland awaited. Five of the ubiquitous LSTs lined up in a row, waiting to load the 417th and several of the single-engined day-fighter squadrons who were also moving closer to the fighting. They 417th drove their dozens of assorted transports – 2½ ton trucks (the famous 'deuce and a half'), jeeps, weapons carriers, even a couple of motorcycles – into the cavernous hold. The men's accommodation was an afterthought, and they were scattered among the trucks and wherever a spare corner could be found.

The aircraft took off for the last time from Borgo and made the brief hop to the squadron's new home at Le Vallon at the mouth of the Rhône valley, the great pathway into southern Germany, about 20 miles north-east of the large port city of Marseilles which was one of only two ports capable of handling large shipping. Its importance to the Allied war effort was huge. Both the Allies and the Germans knew that and the latter would try desparately to close it through air raids. The 417th would soon be back in the business of harbour and convoy protection for this crucial gateway.

After the squadron had been packed aboard, the LST's 'critical' cargo was loaded. Hundreds upon hundreds of Supermarine Spitfire belly tanks were stacked on the upper deck of the ungainly transport ship. The famous Spitfire was providing both air and ground attack cover as the Allied advanced and needed the tanks to continue operations. Veterans recall the horrendous noise caused by the belly tanks rolling to and fro as the LST lumbered across the Mediterranean to the beach of St Raphael.

After a day waiting for the 'important cargo' to be unloaded, the 417th's motor convoy set out for Le Vallon. Once again, the squadron found itself setting up camp and operating from a bleak location. The official history reported:

Upon arrival at Le Vallon airport, a barren, depressing field close to a range of dangerous mountains [the Alpilles], the men erected the tent area approximately one and half miles north-east of the runway and [flight] line. Although care was taken to place the tents behind the shelter of a long windbreak by closely planted fir trees, French officials and civilians warned that when the winter Mistral began, the tents would be blown into the sea, thirty miles distant; however, there was no alternative to this arrangement. The closest town was 11 miles away and transportation to and from the field to the town would have been too great a strain on our limited means.

This constant wind developed during autumn and winter into a phenomenon called the Mistral, a well-known sustained gale of 50mph, sometimes more. It became another daily fact of life for both flying and living. Pilot 'Dirty' Dalton remembers:

> I got pretty good at crosswind landings in the Beau, I had to. Our field at Le Vallon, had a dirt runway lying east-west. The predominant weather there was a strong wind from the north called 'le Mistral'. When I say strong, I mean in the 40-60 knot range, sometimes more!
>
> We still had to fly our assigned missions no matter the weather, so I just had to get good at handling the crosswind. Sometimes, when the weather was so bad during the day that it grounded the single-engine guys, we even had to send up planes to cover their patrol areas.

The strong winds played havoc with work on the fighters and the delicate radar sets. Dust and dirt blew into every nook and crevice, often clogging the vacuum tubes and wiring of these first-generation radars. Air Force headquarters decided that the 417th needed a protected hangar rather than the tents and tarpaper shacks they were using to cut down on the failure rates. A construction battalion descended on the base and began erecting a steel girder and heavy canvas hangar big enough to hold two Beaufighters. The door was to the south, opposite the Mistral's path, to cut down on wind-blown dirt. Unfortunately, the builders did not pour a concrete foundation, relying on the weight of the large hangar to hold it down. It was a poor decision because three days after they finished it, the Mistral swept down the Rhône Valley and picked up the hangar like a child's toy and crumpled it into ruins. The squadron returned to their makeshift maintenance accommodation and carried on with business.

Even daily living was at the mercy of the Mistral. Pilot Bob Condon described the ordeal of getting from the officers' tent area to the mess tent. The tents were backed into a line of trees to provide some relief from the wind, but to provide access a road had to be cut through the trees. 'Crossing that road during a blow could be interesting, especially when there was ice. At such times it was necessary to crawl across the gap in the road.'

CHAPTER 9

By 15 September, the squadron was back in business, searching the skies and scouring the ground for German military forces. Once again, the Germans sent in reconnaissance aircraft to sniff out what was happening in the port, but this time, instead of coming in right above the waves, they went to the other extreme and tried very high-level snooping. On the night of 25 September, pilot Captain Alex McQueen was vectored onto the first target for the squadron in France. It was friendly but still needed to be destroyed. One of the barrage balloons, the large, helium-filled blimps tethered over ships and important ground targets to discourage low-level attacks by the *Luftwaffe*, had broken loose from its moorings and was floating around the Rhône valley. With all the Allied aircraft conducting missions in the area, it was a real hazard and needed to be removed.

GCI vectored him into the area, but McQueen could not see the target. After three passes along the path where ground radar said the balloon was, he broke off and returned to base, irritated at missing some target practice. After landing, however, he and his ground crew discovered just how close he had come to the errant balloon. He actually hit its cable, dangling below the gas bag, snagged it and towed it for nearly 15 miles before the cable snapped again. McQueen landed trailing some 4,000ft of 1-in wire. Another patrol finally shot down the annoying balloon.

The next night, Lieutenant J.W. 'Woody' Grange and his R/O, Lieutenant John Sunyar, suffered the first of an incredible string of 417th engine failures. The Beau, unable to maintain altitude, steadily descended into the Mediterranean. Grange did a credible job of putting it down, and the crew was picked up within hours by Air-Sea Rescue.

That incident was followed by another tragedy. The long-serving crew of Captain John Lee and Lieutenant Leonard Potter crashed while conducting an NFT off Marseilles. Both were killed instantly. The crash was witnessed by the operations officer, Captain Dick McCray, flying as wingman. McCray circled the slowly dissipating splash where the Beaufighter had gone in, but it was hopeless. Both men were dead.

That same night, Grange again suffered engine failure. This time, both engines failed and Grange and Sunyar baled out over the mountains. After several days in the wilderness, they returned to the squadron. Unbelievably, they lost both engines on a subsequent flight and ditched again.

This last accident finally pushed the R/O over the edge. On another flight soon after their third disaster, the low fuel pressure indicator illuminated in Grange's cockpit. Normally, this was a transient indication and went away quickly as the fuel pumps built up pressure in the tanks. This time, however, the light stayed on. Over the intercom, Grange told Sunyar, 'We are going in' meaning 'We are returning to base.' Sunyar, spring-loaded to leave the unreliable Beaufighter at the first sign of trouble, took the comment to mean 'We are crashing' and promptly baled out!

Safely back at Le Vallon, Grange shut the engines down and left the aircraft. He stood by, waiting for Sunyar to get out via his hatch in the back, but the R/O never appeared. Upon further investigation, Grange and the crew chief discovered Sunyar's headphones and oxygen mask dangling, but no Sunyar. They had no idea where he was. Some hours later, the squadron received a phone call from the mother superior of the nunnery in the town of Istres, around 10 miles from the airfield. She told the duty officer that she had one of the Americans with her and would they please come and get him. Sunyar later explained why he had baled out and reported the series of mishaps that followed his jump.

Most aircrews wore chest-type parachutes; there was a harness with the packed parachute clipped to it. In a Beau, however, the chest parachute prevented the R/O from leaning forward and seeing the scope, so he kept it to the side, ready to clip on in an emergency. Sunyar managed to get only one clip of his chute attached before he jumped. When the parachute blossomed, he had no control over it and swung wildly to the ground. The silk canopy snagged on the corner of the nunnery and he hung there.

The nuns, after four years of brutal Nazi occupation, thought he was a German and soon began berating him in a most un-Christian like manner. Sunyar was eventually able to explain that he was one of the good guys and calmed them down.

In the words of some of the other crews, Sunyar became a 'wild man' after that. Nervous, twitching, and drinking heavily, he eventually survived his tour and went home in early 1945.

The run of tragedies continued when Second Lieutenant Jack Devore and his R/O, Second Lieutenant William Grinnell, were pursuing a Ju 188. During a long chase, the crew suddenly radioed that they were baling out, and gave a position report. Nothing further was ever heard from the crew and no trace was ever found.

The almost endless litany of accidents continued with First Lieutenant Joe Davis's crash in Beaufighter ND296. He was taking the aircraft up for a test hop following maintenance, a routine procedure to verify that it performed satisfactorily before sending it out on operational missions. He lost an engine and crashed while trying to land. The Beaufighter burst into flames and Davis was badly burned before he could be rescued.

Failing engines claimed two more Beaufighters, one sent to look for the other. In the first incident, Lieutenants Berryhill and Rodgers along with their crew chief, Staff Sergeant Anderton, disappeared on a flight to Dijon. Lieutenants Howard and Mangone, flying with their crew chief, Staff Sergeant Schmitt, to search for the first crew, blew a rod in their starboard engine and crash-landed in Lyon. During his final approach, Howard's other engine also failed, necessitating a wheels-up belly landing. All three men escaped, shaken but unharmed. His accident report read:

At 1400, I was at angels 5 when the starboard engine suddenly cut out and caught again, only to keep spitting and knocking with unusual vigor.

All engine instruments registered normal, but being near the field I elected to make a high, long approach. I lowered the undercarriage, but the port wheel failed to come down. I lifted the starboard [gear] again and lowered the gear handle a second time to no avail. I made an attempt to use the emergency system and pumped all the way while approaching the field but didn't have enough time to get the gear down.

Being committed to the landing, I judged it impossible to go around on one engine. As I came to the end of the runway, I warned the crew of the coming belly landing, cut the switches and came in. The plane hit smoothly and dragged a long way. It did not catch fire.

This unrelenting string of aircraft failures took its toll on both air and ground crews. The flyers began to dread taking the unreliable Beaus aloft. If their own aeroplane could kill them just flying along, what chance did they have going into combat where the demands made on the craft were magnified?

The crew chiefs, engine mechanics and airframe technicians were also down and depressed. They slaved long hours trying to keep the weary fighters in the air and thought they did a good job. When a crew failed to return the nagging thought of 'What did I do wrong?' haunted them.

An engine failure at any time is cause for immediate concern to a pilot. In a single-engined aircraft, it obviously becomes very quiet very quickly. Immediate pilot reactions include trying to identify why the engine failed, and attempting to restart the engine, while seeking an open place to set the aircraft down if he cannot fire up the engine again. A twin-engined aircraft immediately begins yawing or crabbing to one side. The pilot has to apply immediate rudder to counteract the yaw; soon his leg muscles begin trembling under the strain. Immediate actions also include identifying the cause of the failure, trying to restart the engine, and since the Beaufighter could rarely hold altitude on one engine, also peering out for a nice, smooth place to set the aircraft down. And this usually happened at night, so everything had to be done by feel.

Captain Dick McCray suffered this fate while on a mission that involved crossing the French Alps into the very northern part of Italy. Losing an engine, he faced a long flight home, threading his aircraft through the towering mountains with their peaks above him. Good piloting and adroit radar use by his R/O to paint the openings between the peaks enabled him to make it home. These engine failures almost brought the squadron to its knees. By the time the cause was found, the 417th had the highest accident rate in the entire Air Force. Numerous crews, shaken by near calamities and seeing their comrades close brushes, asked to be relieved from night fighters. After McCray's flight and after several good men had died, the cause of the engine failures was finally discovered. McCray followed a hunch about the fuel the squadron was using and found that the 100 octane aviation fuel delivered by tanker ship to huge holding tanks in Marseilles was pumped into 55-gallon barrels before being delivered to the squadron. The barrels were stored on the docks with their lids off, so rainwater collected in them and the dockers didn't bother to empty the barrels before filling them with fuel. The Beaus were therefore getting watered down fuel and the results were tragically demonstrated. But fuel was in extremely short supply in the entire European theatre, so condemning the fuel meant not flying at all, an unthinkable option. After this discovery, therefore, it had to be laboriously filtered before filling the fighters' tanks before each flight.

Late in 1944, the new crewmen, Second Lieutenant Graybill and Flight Officer Klein were killed while on an orientation flight. They were racing along at low level when they struck some power lines. The aircraft reared up and then slammed into the ground, tumbling into a pile of flaming junk, and killing the two men instantly

New crews kept replacing old ones and dead ones in the endless round of personnel rotation. In today's world of highly regimented training, and documentation of that training, the introduction of new aircrew to the Beaufighter seems incredible. For example, Dalton reported to the squadron fresh from night-fighter training in the states, where he had last flown the P-70. His description of his check-out in the Beau is illuminating. 'After many hours of cockpit drill – sitting blindfolded in the cockpit until I could readily identify every switch, knob, and control by touch, I took my first flight in the Beau. Since there was only one pilot's seat, the instructor crouched behind the pilot and gave instructions.' Like 'Doc' Katzberg, Dalton's mentor perched on the ammo cans behind the pilot and observed his performance in the unfamiliar aircraft. 'After only twenty minutes in the local area, my check pilot, a captain, told me to land, I was qualified.' Placed in the operational line-up after this flight, Dalton crewed with newly arrived Flight Officer, later Second Lieutenant, William Work as his R/O.

'Doc' Katzberg's time to go home finally came. In December 1944, he went to a replacement organization, eventually being assigned to escort some wounded GIs home on a troop ship. He took care of their medical needs on the voyage home until they docked back in New York. After nineteen months overseas, he was back in America.

The 417th was lucky to get another good flight surgeon in his place. Like Katzberg, Dr Marvin Weinberg was a character in his own right. An accomplished pianist, he made friends with a well-to-do family in the Le Vallon area, helping them and discussing art and music with them. So great was this family's affection for him that they loaned him a baby grand piano. Many 417th veterans of that time recall the beautifully played classical piano tunes emanating from Weinberg's tent in the late hours of the night. R/O John Sunyar, himself an accomplished violinist, often accompanied Weinberg.

Besides tending to the health and morale of the men, Weinberg developed an intense interest in the workings of the still new technology of radar. He spent hours in the radar shop, watching the men working on the sets, asking questions and taking notes. It was not long before he could be seen on the flight line, working on sets himself.

Throughout the trials of unreliable aircraft and the turmoil of constant personnel rotation, the 417th continued to carry the fight to the enemy. Lieutenants Allen and Grinnell scored a 'probable' against a Ju 188. Allen's combat report stated:

Our a/c was airborne at 1755 hrs. At 1800 hrs, we went on patrol with MATURE [a GCI station] in the area of St Tropez, at an altitude of 8,000ft. At 1852 hrs, we passed into MIMIC's area. MIMIC vectored us onto a 'bogey' along with a descent to low level. MIMIC informed us 'bogey' was 10 miles south of Nice doing orbits right on the deck.

We accelerated to 290mph heading east. Obtained AI contact at 4 miles, 'bogey' doing 300mph, at altitudes ranging from 100-500ft. At 1930 hrs, MIMIC reported that we and the 'bogey' were too low to see and they could offer us no further help. 'Bogey' was heading 040 degrees dead ahead of us. We were at 1,000ft. By this time, both a/c were over the Italian coast heading north-east. 'Bogey' began climbing to 9,000ft where we obtained visual at 500ft range, 20 degrees above.

We closed in to 100ft and identified 'bogey' as Ju 188, then dropped back to 400ft and fired a long burst from dead astern, 15 degrees below bandit. Observed high explosive strikes on rear fuselage just forward of tailplane. Bandit fired a very short burst of tracer without result and fell off to port in a steep spiral dive, near vertical, in excess of 4,000ft per minute rate of descent. Visual was held and we followed bandit earthward, firing long and short bursts.

At 4,000ft altitude, bandit showed no sign of pulling out of dive and went into a cloud deck. We did not follow into clouds as we were unfamiliar with the surrounding country. Position at the time was unknown, but approximately 10 – 15 miles south-east of Cremona, Italy. We flew south-west for 20 minutes, contacted MIMIC and resumed patrol.

Enemy a/c's rate and manner of descent over mountainous terrain justified this aircrew's claim of one Ju 188 probably destroyed.

Long-time 417th pilot Ted Deakyne finally got his first kill in November 1944. The squadron's diary records: 'At last! Deakyne finally got a Jerry "destroyed"'. Having flown Beaufighters and Mosquitoes with the RAF, then joining the 417th and coming back to Beaufighters again. This happened when Jerry was taking night photos of Marseilles and Toulon.'

The squadron also finally got the reconnaissance aircraft that had been investigating the harbour and forces around it. In numerous attempts to catch it, they had suffered some heart-breaking failures. 'Dirty' Dalton was unable to get high enough in a worn-out Beau to make contact with the enemy plane on one of his early patrols. So difficult was it to climb the old Beaus to altitude that the RAF had to send in the much more capable and modern Mosquito night fighter. Light, nimble and extremely fast, the 'Mossie' had become the standard British night fighter, replacing their own Beaufighters in that role.

Besides providing top cover for the 417th, Dalton recalls, the Mosquitoes served as an unexpected supply source for the squadron. Yankee ingenuity combined the accomplishment of the mission with acquiring badly needed spare parts.

> Since we couldn't get this guy in our Beaufighters, the RAF sent in a Mosquito night fighter to take care of him. When the 'Mossie' landed at our field, we took the crew off for some chatting and dinner in the field mess. Meanwhile, our maintenance guys swapped out the 'Mossie's' landing gear – wheels and all – with one of our tired Beau sets. They were the same wheels so it worked.
>
> It wasn't just a prank or to be obnoxious. As I said, parts for the Beau were non-existent in the US supply system. We had a squadron 'hack', a worn-out B-25 that we used to search all over the Mediterranean for parts.
>
> The Brits were fairly good-natured about the switch and even shot down the pesky photo intruder so everybody got something from the deal.

Bob Condon, one of the second generation of replacement pilots to fill the 417th's roster, shares some other experiences of both the RAF visit and the primitive life of a combat squadron:

> The RAF guys came in to get this high-flying Jerry, but since the field at Le Vallon was dirt and rocks, every time he accelerated the Mosquito down the runway, he'd throw rocks up through his rudder and elevators [which were fabric covered], punching holes in the control surfaces, making his aircraft u/s.
>
> While they were with us, they had a fire in their tent. Poor guys lost everything except a dress uniform and one flying boot. Our fire truck was broken so there was nothing we could do to stop the blaze.

The cause of the fire was rats. The officers' tent area was on a former alfalfa field and there was plenty of trampled forage for them, so they made themselves at home in the tents. Bored young men decided that only rat genocide would do. With more enthusiasm than thought, they poured 100 octane fuel down every suspected rat hole that could be found, and fired flares into the holes. The rats, crazed and on fire, poured out of their holes and through the tents, setting many of them on fire, including the visiting Mosquito crew's.

'While it was burning', says Condon, "Dirty" Dalton and I were standing nearby watching. One of the Limeys' pistols got hot enough to cook off a round and passed between Dirty and me. We looked wide-eyed at each other and left the vicinity at a quick-step.'

Condon describes some of his other, less dramatic experiences.

> Bathing was a problem. There was only a Lister bag of drinking water, not enough to take a bath or shower. A tin helmet full of hot water was the usual solution, but about once every six weeks we had access to the public showers of a nearby town.
>
> For some reason, it seemed we always got there right after the whole French army had finished their showers. The stalls were full of dirty, soapy water – ankle deep – and they never drained well.
>
> As a result, we often discussed as to whether we were cleaner when we got through or when we started.

He tells this anecdote about one of the original pilots still in the 417th, Alex McQueen.

> It was the dead of winter and McQueen decided he needed to clean his GI clothing. There weren't any civilians coming around in the bad weather or maybe he was just too cheap to pay the minuscule fee they charged.
>
> Anyway, he decided to clean his clothes in 100 octane gas. He got a bucketful from the flight line and proceeded to handwash his pants and shirt on a table in the middle of the tent row.
>
> There wasn't much odd about that except he was smoking a cigar at the time. The rest of us, watching from a distance, expected him and his clothes to go up at any time. What we

didn't know, and he did, was that a strong breeze was keeping the gas fumes away from his stogie.

His check-out in the Beaufighter was typical of most new guys.

At first, we were somewhat put out by the appearance of the aged, over-used fighters. The Beaus were showing a lot of wear and tear. Several were still flying because so many parts had been cannibalized from others. One of them was impossible to trim up to level, forward flight. It always flew slightly sideways when trimmed to go straight. Another had one engine that had no propeller-feathering capability because it was too old a model from before feathering was incorporated.

However, knowing what the 'old heads' had done in them, we were ready and eager to learn.

I was the first of our little group to check out in the Beau. One of the senior pilots, Ted Deakyne, took me up as a passenger for my initial ride and having reached 3,000ft altitude, he started to crawl out of the pilot's seat! I yelled out, 'What are you doing?' and he replied that he was going to let me climb into his seat and take over.

For those unfamiliar with the Beaufighter, there is a sturdy steel pipe athwart the cockpit, right behind the pilot's shoulders. Getting into the pilot's seat required climbing over this pipe and lowering oneself into the seat. Passengers riding in the front of the airplane stood behind the pipe on the hatch that was used to enter the front area.

Now getting out of the pilot's seat was neat. One disconnected from all the equipment – radio headset plug-in, oxygen mask, seatbelt, etc. – and grabbed a pair of the fore and aft pipes on the ceiling of the space behind the cockpit and did a backward somersault on the hatch!

Captain Deakyne didn't do the backward somersault trick, but just slid out in the reverse of the entry motion, thus able to keep an eye on our altitude throughout the manoeuvre. He moved over and allowed me to climb, feet first, into the pilot's seat.

I checked out the Beau's stall and slow-speed flight conditions, including a simulated landing with gear and flaps down, and proceeded to take it back to the airfield and make a

decent landing. The unfamiliar air brakes and their thumb lever operation caused me no trouble.

Part of the familiarization that Captain Deakyne showed me was that the take-off was made with wide open throttles. In fact, it was a common saying that for take-off, the throttles were pushed to the firewall and bent over to stay there and the pilot then devoted both hands to getting the plane airborne without a ground loop! Getting the tail up to gain rudder control rather than brakes steering was part of the process.

Condon recalls some of the stupid mistakes made by pilots that livened up camp life, including a new man, Hoffman, who took off in a Beaufighter.

He took off in the usual manner, shoved both throttles forward, then devoted both hands to pushing the yoke forward to get the tail up and gain rudder effectiveness. Unfortunately, Hoffman was mashing the gun firing button down the whole length of the runway.

Another pilot yanked the gear handle up as soon as the wheels left the dirt. The Beau's Hercules engines hiccuped and settled down briefly onto the retracting gear. The gear was smashed into a partially retracted mess. It would not come up so the pilot, Flight Officer Harding, could not belly land, and trying to land on the stumps was considered too dangerous. Ordered to bale out, Harding flew alongside the runway and jumped. The squadron diary records, 'A "successful" exit was made from the a/c, or at least it appeared at the time to be so. At the time he left the aircraft, something "shiny" was also seen to leave the a/c.' Weapons carriers, jeeps, and the ambulance all followed FO Harding and when the ambulance arrived at his landing place, he was found to be very seriously injured and unconscious. Bob Condon recalls this accident.

We found him hanging in a tree, unconscious. We took him down and when he didn't regain consciousness, took him to a hospital. Turned out he had a basal skull fracture. When we visited him in the hospital later, he was severely cross-eyed, but with good prospects for recovery. He got shipped home from there.

CHAPTER 10

As 1944 drew to a close, the rumours of the long-awaited P-61s began surfacing. The other US Beau squadrons had already changed their equipment; the 414th, still in Italy, acquired its first 'Black Widows' in December 1943; the 415th got theirs soon after the New Year; and the 416th, surprisingly, turned in their tired Beaufighters for de Havilland Mk XXX Mosquitoes, the only US night-fighter squadron to get the 'wooden wonder'. The 12th Air Force, however, decided to keep the 417th's Beaus until more P-61s could be obtained. With fresh squadrons like the 422nd NFS and others pouring into Britain in P-61s, the wait would be substantial. The 417th made do, yet again.

Every contact with the enemy was fraught with danger for the Americans in their hand-me-down Beaufighters. Every interception meant the risk of death or permanent disfigurement, but still the crews went out. Every 'confirmed destroyed', 'probably destroyed', and 'damaged' claim was one more chip knocked from Germany's fighting capability. Finally, in December 1944, the squadron received its most important mission, one that put the greatest dent in the Nazi government's armour.

The men, shivering in the cold, were necessarily concerned with the day-to-day prospect of staying alive. For the 'big picture' men in the halls of power, the fact that Germans were storing looted gold and other treasures meant either the possibility of the war spreading to other areas or the re-emergence of a Fourth Reich after this war was over. Both were unthinkable. It was into this intrigue that the 417th was thrown.

As early as 1942, the British government had begun trying to isolate and account for the hundreds of millions of dollars in gold stolen from the treasuries of occupied Europe. Germany, as it rolled through the various countries, absconded with the wealth of each.

Belgium lost the most, with $223 million in gold taken, but the Netherlands also lost more than $100 million. France, Italy, Czechoslovakia, Poland, Luxembourg and other countries also had tens of millions taken. By 1944, the total take was estimated at over $500 million – and this was just in gold bullion. The value of art stolen from both national and private holdings added up to several more hundreds of millions of dollars. Much of this wealth went into Swiss banks where it effectively disappeared, but significant amounts found its way into other neutral countries, such as Spain.

As the American, British, and French forces drove toward Paris and Rheims, the Soviet Union's Red Army was pressing into Germany from the east. Even the most optimistic Nazi probably realized that the end was near. The Allied leadership, particularly those concerned with post-war reconstruction, certainly realized. In fact, the US Treasury Department's Foreign Economic Administration developed a programme, *Project Safehaven*, designed to root out and neutralize German industrial and commercial power wherever it might be found. It sought to deny the transfer of German industrial and fiscal capital to neutral countries, to escape the Allied plan for confiscation and reparation. If this transfer happened, the economic base of the Nazis would remain largely intact and could act as a power base from which die-hards could build a resurgent Fourth Reich for another generation. *Safehaven*'s objective was to deny this possibility.

Thousands of truckloads of German gold, captured or stolen foreign currency, looted art and other treasures of occupied Europe were spirited into neutral countries. Spain received a sizeable share of this flow of capital although the exact value is vague. However, by August 1944, the land access routes from German-occupied territory to Spain were finally severed. The only way to ship stolen goods was via either air or sea. The Allied navies controlled the sea, but the night fighters were responsible for stopping the airborne couriers.

Radar control centres situated along the French Riviera

reported an unknown air track originating in the areas between Strasbourg, which was still occupied by the Germans and Stuttgart. Aircraft flew westward starting around 9 p.m. until the radar plot faded in Spain. Then, a contact was picked up heading in the opposite direction in the early morning, between 3.30 and 4.30. Both radar plots were detected at extremely low level throughout the flight.

The job of intercepting these flights was first assigned to one of the 417th's sister squadrons, the 415th NFS, then based at Dijon and using the codenamed of *Boxcar*. Because the Germans had a very efficient radio interception capability, called the 'Y Service' by the Allies, the 415th had to develop a radio-silent method of intercepting this strange flight. If the usual GCI to fighter radio transmissions were detected, the Y Service could warn the low-level flier and enable it to turn back.

The Beau squadrons, in yet another reorganization, had by this stage of the war been assigned to the US 64th Fighter Wing. The 64th was primarily responsible for the GCI and associated fighter squadrons in southern France. Its senior controller, Major Julius Goldstein, Captain George Schiff, the radar officer, and 415th's commanding officer, Captain Harold Augsperger, devised a plan to intercept the aircraft using only coded transmissions from the GCI station. This method of 'broadcast' control is still used by modern air forces.

In this tactic, the GCI station gives the location of a 'bogey' in relation to a pre-briefed reference point called a 'bull's eye'. By this method, the GCI could give all the tactical data needed by the fighter, but allowed the fighter to remain silent. The pilot and R/O plotted the call from the GCI station, for example, 'Bogey, bull's eye, 340 for 20, heading 200, 200, low.' This meant, 'The target is 20 miles north-west of the reference point, heading south-west, speed 200 knots, at low level.' Referencing their own map, the crew could fly to the predicted intercept point and scan the skies using their own AI radar.

On 27 September, Augsperger and his R/O, Second Lieutenant Austin Petry, were patrolling along the expected line of the westbound flight. They did not have long to wait. At 8.07 p.m. the GCI site, Delaware picked up a 'bogey' and within two minutes identified the track as hostile, having received no friendly

IFF, knowing that no Allied aircraft were flying in the area where the radar blip appeared, and seeing that it was on the Germany – Spain run.

At 8.10 p.m. Petry obtained AI contact and vectored Augsperger onto the target. After more than twenty minutes, Augsperger broke radio silence to confirm that the mystery aircraft was an enemy saying, 'Eureka! It's a Jerry.' He picked enough details of the low-flying plane to identify it as a Focke-Wolf FW 200 Condor, the famous German long-range transport and reconnaissance aircraft. He fired at it, and it went down in an enormous fireball, exploding on impact with the ground.

The next day, Allied intelligence experts sifted through the wreckage, confirming the value of the cargo and the fact that parts of the Nazi government was, in fact, attempting to transfer money and other valuables into Spanish banks for future use, either personal or governmental. After this flight, the *Luftwaffe* only attempted the Spanish run in the most abysmally bad weather on the darkest nights.

The winter of 1944/5 was the worst in a generation and the *Luftwaffe* took advantage of the opportunity to crank up the flights to Spain again. Allied intelligence briefed the 417th's commanding officer and intelligence officer on 'Barcelona Charlie's' renewed activity in mid-December. In a schedule reminiscent of their Corsican adventures chasing 'Bedcheck Charlies', the 417th laid on additional patrols to search for the treasure flights. These patrols were in addition to the regular harbour and convoy patrols, night-intruder sorties, and crew training flights. All these requirements stretched the maintenance shops to the limit, but rarely did a flight have to be cancelled due to unserviceable aircraft. Even though the long-awaited P-61 Black Widows had finally made it into combat in Europe with several other night-fighter squadrons, among them the 422nd and 425th, the 417th was to be the last to get the new aircraft and had to soldier on with the venerable Beaus scrounged from other squadrons until the supply ran out.

Bob Condon made himself *persona non grata* for a few days after picking up a cast-off British Beaufighter in Italy. Dropped off by the hard-working squadron B-25, he thought he would be able to just sign for the aircraft, fire it up and fly back to Le

Vallon. It did not work out that way. After accepting the aircraft from the RAF squadron, he found that its battery was dead. He had to badger the RAF line chief for several days to get a replacement. The British NCO finally relented, if only to get him to go away. Condon replaced the battery and cranked the two Hercules engines, only to find major problems with their exhaust systems. Rather than be stuck at the RAF field again and at the mercy of the uncooperative NCO, he struggled aloft and made the flight back to the 417th. He knew that his own maintenance men could solve the problem and he could relax among friends.

However, his reception was less than pleasant. The commanding officer, the operations officer and even the line chief, Earl Wetherald, now promoted to senior master sergeant, all read Condon the riot act for bringing in another old Beau in such bad shape. They were angry because if the squadron could use up all the Beaus in its inventory, they could re-equip with the P-61s that much faster. Condon's efforts just delayed the long-awaited day when Northrop's sleek, powerful fighter graced the 417th's flight line.

Despite its desire to obtain shiny, new aeroplanes, the squadron still had missions to fly, including stopping the flights to Spain. After dozens of these patrols and a few fleeting radar contacts, 'Duff' Campbell and Bob McCullen made AI contact, and pursued, sighted and shot down 'Barcelona Charlie', thus further hampering the Nazis' last attempts to retain a grip on a post-war future. The crew and the 417th did not know it at the time, but this victory was probably their greatest contribution to winning the war. Incidentally, it was also the last confirmed victory any American crew would make in the decrepit Beaufighters.

Hitler now unleashed his last-ditch massive offensive through the Ardennes Forest area that became to be called the Battle of the Bulge. One of the conditions the Germans counted on for the success of this armoured plunge into the Allied lines was the typically atrocious weather that would keep the Allied air forces grounded. This crew, along with most of the other night fighters, played an important part in defeating this final German offensive in the West.

As the Germans advanced and then receded, Major Larson, the commanding officer, flew the squadron B-25 to the airfield designated A-78 near Florennes, Belgium, just after the turn of the year. Accompanying him were three flights of the squadron's Beaufighters, leaving Le Vallon empty of aircraft. For nearly three weeks, this detachment endured frigid temperatures and heavy snowfall in what turned out to be a frustrating, fruitless attempt to provide air cover for the Allied response to the German assault. With the onset of reasonable flying weather, other more effective ground attack aircraft like the American P-47 Thunderbolt and British Typhoon were able to take to the skies and blunt the massive offensive, so the 417th returned to Le Vallon, bitter and frustrated at not being able to contribute to the effort.

While the aircraft were deployed away from their home field, there was not much for those left behind to do. In probably the saddest, most useless death of a 417th member, one of the original cadre of pilots, Captain Alex McQueen was shot and killed while sitting in a café in the town of Nimes. A group of black enlisted men was also drinking. McQueen, always cantankerous, especially when intoxicated, kept making racist comments. Eventually, one of the troops drilled McQueen through the chest with a .45 calibre round from his pistol. McQueen died instantly from an American's bullet and a big mouth, having survived over forty missions against the Germans.

CHAPTER 11

As 1945 progressed, the pace of the war picked up. In February, the commander of the XII Tactical Air Command, Brigadier General Gilbert Meyers, visited the squadron and presented medals. First Lieutenant Campbell and Second Lieutenant McCullen won DFCs and an Air Medal. The commanding officer Major Larson, was awarded his second and third clusters to his Air Medal. Major Dick McCray got his second to fifth clusters. Another ten flyers pinned on Air Medals during this ceremony. Meyers later flew a tour of the local area sitting in the R/O's position of a Beaufighter.

It is probably coincidental that at the time of Meyer's visit and flight in a Beau the first of what would be a large change in personnel and equipment occurred. In preparation for getting P-61s, civilian radar technician J.A. Pesler arrived to instruct the radar-shop troops in the new SCR-720 C model used by the Black Widow.

Before the first Widow arrived, however, new pilots and R/Os arriving in the squadron found themselves with little to do. Since the end of the war was in sight, the Air Force had developed a rotation system for veteran aircrews to return home. They had to fly a minimum number of hours to complete a tour, so the older pilots and R/Os hogged all the flying time they could to meet those minimums. Those last few hours could be as dangerous as any, however. For example, on 16 March 1945, a Beau piloted by First Lieutenant Howard finished its patrol and was vectored back to base. However, a layer of fog rolled in and completely socked in the field. Howard radioed that he could see the runway lights when directly overhead, but as soon as he flew out to set up for a straight-in final run, everything disappeared. Since he was fast running out of fuel and options, the 417th lined up their motley assortment of ground transports and turned on their lights in the direction of the runway while simultaneously lighting a large bonfire at the opposite end. With this extra help, Howard made what the squadron history deemed 'a raunchy, but highly satisfactory landing'.

R/O Tom Hart joined the squadron in January 1945 and recalls sitting around for a month and a half before getting his first flight in a Beaufighter due to the rush of the 'old heads' to complete their tours. During this down time, Hart had numerous opportunities to travel around France. He recalls talking to RAF radar controller Flying Officer George Parrot, the same officer who had trained the 417th squadron in the mysteries of GCI back in England in 1943. By now, Parrot commanded a mobile GCI station located on a spit of land opposite Monte Carlo. On the east side of the bay, his German counterpart had his GCI station. In an almost comical situation, each side waved to the other when outside, neither wishing to call in either air or ground fire on the other since the end of the war was clearly in sight. Indeed, Parrot sometime swam in the Monte Carlo harbour where his German opposite went as well.

Parrot's fame lives on. During World War II, the radio code word for IFF was 'Cockerel'. 'Strangle cockerel' meant 'Turn your IFF off' and 'Make your cockerel crow' meant 'Turn on your IFF'. 'Cockerel' was such a strange term for US aircrew, who called a male chicken a 'cock', the term morphed into 'Parrot', since everyone knew what a parrot was. The term 'Strangle parrot' and similar others are still used today in Western fighter aviation. Thus does RAF controller George Parrot's legacy live on.

As February closed, Second Lieutenant Bob Condon with his R/O, Second Lieutenant Dick Cornwall, had their first combat after arriving back in November the previous year. GCI vectored them onto the trail of a fast manoeuvring target. Cornwall then took over the intercept, guiding Condon's eyes onto the 'bogey' until Condon could identify it as a Messerschmitt Me 410 Hornisse (Hornet). It was a phenomenal German night fighter, fast, manoeuvrable and heavily armed. More than a match for

Condon's Beaufighter, it would have made short work of the American if Condon had muffed the attack. He did not.

The 410 was flying low over the Mediterranean; Condon had developed his own theory about how to take down such a low flyer. He reckoned that trying to get underneath an adversary was a good way to fly into the sea since it only took a second's distraction to plough into the unforgiving waves. Instead, he flew flat out at full throttle, opening fire at the same level. Although both he and Cornwall saw their shells strike home repeatedly, they could not verify that the Me-410 went down so they could only claim a 'probable'.

Condon also had a unique way of preparing for such a mission. While most crews conducting an NFT in preparation for a later flight contented themselves with climbing to altitude, checking out the aircraft and its systems, Condon says:

> My favourite place to test the radar altimeter was the Rhône River. I would fly low along the twisting, tree-bordered course and when the props picked up water from the river, I was exactly 10ft above the water.
>
> To test out the guns, I would fire at some target on the beach. There was a deserted tower at one particular spot that made a good target. I also found a large round black ball washed up on the beach and made one short run at it. Luckily, I didn't hit it, because as I passed over it at low altitude, I realized it was a mine. If it had exploded from my firing, it would have blown my Beau to smithereens!

A few nights later, Dick McCray was entering the Le Vallon airfield traffic pattern after a boring three-hour patrol. The GCI station Dogleg picked up a contact at 24,000ft and asked if McCray could investigate. McCray tried to climb to that height, but the straining Hercules engines were not up to the task and McCray could not get it above 22,000ft. Whoever was flying 2,000ft higher was safe that night.

In March, the long-awaited arrival of the squadron's first Northrop P-61 Black Widow occurred. By the end of the month, the rest of the unit's new mounts had also arrived and the Beaus were unceremoniously cast aside. The first P-61, serial number 42-39420, represented the best that American technology could produce and the 'Widow' was a coveted possession for both air and ground crews.

Crew chief Earl Hissett called the P-61 a 'great aircraft, and a maintenance dream'. With parts and tools designed to US specifications and spares already flowing in the supply system, besides being newer and less abused than the old Beaus, one can easily understand why the engineering troops and mechanics were elated.

Although the entire squadron was pleased to receive the new planes, they were also saddened by the loss of one of the original members and a friend to all in First Sergeant 'Doc' Hockman. He went home on the 16th; everyone was glad for him that he was going home, but sad to see him go. Tom Luke, the personnel specialist who had joined the squadron back in Corsica stepped into his role. He was kept busy as the pace of life was about to pick up dizzying speed.

First, at the end of the month, the squadron stood down while all the crews checked out in the P-61s. Many of the newer crews were still familiar with the P-61 from their training but the ground crews were the prime concern; they needed time to learn the new equipment. Then in early April, it received orders to move to St Dizier, closer to the advancing Allied lines in central and northern France. They did not stay there long, just over three weeks, but they still managed several dramatic adventures.

At St Dizier a new pilot Lieutenant R.P. Bradford, was making a routine training flight, trying to get up to speed on the Widow so that he could join the operational line-up when he tried a stunt often attempted by young, daring pilots, but one with sometimes tragic consequences if it did not work. He had just about reached flying speed when he pulled the landing gear lever up. When it works, this trick looks good and demonstrates what a 'hot' pilot is at the controls. It is pretty impressive to see a fighter roar down the runway and at the same moment that it breaks ground, see the gear start coming up. Unfortunately, when it does not work, the results can be tragic.

Bradford's P-61 hiccupped for just a second, but that brief hesitation was enough to doom his stunt. The Widow, not climbing, settled back onto the raising gear and crushed them flat. The big racing fighter settled ignominiously onto its belly and slid down the runway for several hundred feet until it stopped in a pile. Bradford scrambled out of the top hatch just as the aircraft, equipped with long-range drop tanks on the wings, lit off with a 'whump' of high octane gas igniting. The crash ambulance recovered Bradford and whisked him off to the hospital, but the P-61 was a complete write-off.

Yet another exuberant newly unleashed Black Widow pilot came within feet of making a big, smoking hole in the ground and taking out many of the men on the ground when he conducted an extremely low-level buzz of the tents. The P-61 built up a tremendous head of steam when it dived; it was much faster and heavier than the Beaufighter and this officially unnamed pilot did not take that into account when he was pulling the Widow out of its dive. The big fighter mushed at the bottom of the pull-out alarmingly, coming within 50ft or so of hitting the tents. As it was, the propwash from the big twin propellers blew down quite a few of the tents.

The 417th even accounted for a German aircraft while on the ground at St Dizier. Pilot Bob Condon recalls the night. A Ju 88, once the scourge of the night skies against the 417th, landed and the crew surrendered to the tower personnel.

> This twin-engined aircraft entered the pattern and the tower gave him a red light [signal meaning not cleared to land]. The aircraft made a go-around on only one engine, the other being dead, and came around again. He landed on the second attempt and ground-looped, collapsing one of the main gear.
>
> A couple of the line guys went out to the plane to help the crew and pulled up short when they saw the swastikas on the tail. Out came two crew members with their hands up.
>
> Seems the pilot was a newly trained *Luftwaffe* pilot who decided enough was enough. He had been sent off to bomb a target nearer the lines with just enough gas to get there and back. St Dizier was as far as he could make it on what gas he did have, so he landed and surrendered just like that.

The next to last big change in April 1945 was the appointment of the squadron's third commanding officer since forming back in Florida in 1942. Major Bill Larsen went back to the United States and the operations officer, Major Dick McCray, assumed command just in time to lead the squadron to its first base in Germany.

Operating from German soil was the last big change of the month. On 23 April, after a two-day truck convoy for most of the ground echelon, the squadron flew its aircraft into Geilbelstadt airfield, coded Y-90 in the Allied plans, located in south-central Germany. The fast-moving front lines were about 40 miles to the east and progressing rapidly as the last German resistance crumbled.

Pilot Bob Condon describes the first night at the new airfield.

The field had been pretty well worked over during the war. The runway was full of bomb craters, there was a smashed Me-262 at the end of the runway, and in the building we used as a ready room that night lay an unexploded 500lb bomb. Altogether a pretty spooky situation.

That evening while we were waiting for the trucks with the rest of the squadron to arrive, I stepped outside to relieve myself under a tree. I had left my hat in the building, and when one of those humungus june-bugs lit in my hair and scrambled around vigorously, I nearly jumped out of my skin!

Bugs aside, the biggest threats faced by the aircrews now was not the *Luftwaffe* but rather being shot at by friendly aircraft or ground fire. On 2 April, the squadron flew its first operational patrols in the Widow, patrolling down the Danube River and over the Allied bridgehead at Ulm. These first patrols were quiet and all aircraft returned home safely.

The next night, however, the squadron lost three Widows in a row, two to American flak and one to pilot error. In the first two losses, P-61 crew Lieutenants T.E. Cartwell, pilot, and H.A Anderson, R/O, were patrolling the Ulm-Dillingen area when the American anti-aircraft batteries clustered around the bridgehead mistook the patrolling night fighter for a marauding German and opened fire. Their P-61 went down in a ball of fire and both men were killed.

They were replaced on patrol by Lieutenants H.J. Allen and Frank Campbell. They too were promptly fired at by the trigger-happy American flak gunners and were lucky to return to base on one engine with holes throughout the fuselage.

The third loss of the night was suffered by pilot Flight Officer George Aubill and his R/O, Lieutenant Tom Hart. The third aircraft to take up patrol over the bridgehead that night, this was their first combat mission. Hart said they briefly had radar contact on what probably turned out to be the first jet fighter of World War II, the stunningly advanced Messerschmitt Me-262. Aubill related that he was listening to GCI give the range decreasing as they crept up on the 'bogey', '2,500 [feet], 2,400, 2,300, 2,200.' Then he heard, '2,300, 2,400, 2,500. ...' So fast was the jet, that it soon outran their P-61, nicknamed 'Lonesome Polecat'.

At the end of the patrol, Aubill returned to the strip at Geibelstadt, but while he was setting up his approach, the runway lights suddenly went out and a searchlight illuminated the aircraft ruining Aubill's night vision and making his landing too dangerous to continue, so he went around for another attempt.

This time the runway lights came on and the searchlight went out so he made a better approach and touched down on the runway. Unfortunately, he had forgotten his landing gear. The 'Lonesome Polecat' screeched down the runway on its belly, the landing gear still firmly in the wheel wells. Aubill recalled that as soon as it settled, he realized what he had done, so he cut the mixtures throttles, and magneto switches off to lessen the chance of fire as they slid down the runway. Both crewmembers got out safely. Aubill tells of the immediate aftermath.

> Only one humorous moment; after we stopped, I stepped over the side from my top hatch to the runway, going aft to Tom's compartment. Since the Widow was on its belly, there was no hatch for Tom to get out of and his compartment was filling with smoke. I took my .45 and tried to hammer open a section as Tom was by now gasping for air. Fortunately, the crash crew arrived almost immediately and 'pickaxed' through to Tom, wounding him superficially from smashing the plexiglass window open.

The 417th's Widow continued patrolling the next two nights but with far less excitement. These turned out to be the last operational missions of the war for the squadron.

CHAPTER 12

On 7 May, 1945, the words every serviceman in Europe longed for arrived. Supreme Allied Headquarters issued the following general order:

> PARA ONE PD ... ALL FORCES WILL CEASE ACTIVE OPERATIONS AT ZERO ZERO ZERO ONE BAKER HOURS, NINE MAY.
> PARA TWO PD EFFECTIVE IMMEDIATELY ALL OFFENSIVE OPERATIONS BY ALLIED EXPEDITIONARY FORCE WILL CEASE AND TROOPS WILL REMAIN IN PRESENT POSITIONS ....

The German Military Command surrendered to the Allied representatives at Rheims on 8 May. VE Day, had at long last arrived.

Immediately, thoughts turned to returning home. When would that be? Would they be sent to help fight in Japan? For a while, no one knew what the future held. Day-to-day living continued while they awaited news of their future.

The long serving and highly regarded maintenance line chief Master Sergeant Earl Weatherald went home on 16 May along with a couple of long-serving pilots, R/Os and enlisted men. The rest just bided their time. Not all the waiting was boring, however. Liberal leaves were granted to many of the men who took advantage of it to see all the places in Europe that they had not yet visited. Many went to Paris to experience the lights and history of that famous city, largely untouched by war damages unlike most of the German cities which were basically just piles of rubble.

R/O Richard 'Dick' Fryklund helped liberate a country during his time off. Seems he was at a bar in Holland talking to an RAF pilot in the days immediately after the ceasefire. The RAF chap was off on a mission to Denmark to check the status of their airports and then to survey the Danish dairy industry with an eye to re-establishing that trade between Britain and Denmark as soon as possible. Having nothing else to do, Fryklund asked if he could go along, to which the RAF man agreed. The next day, they landed at Copenhagen, not really sure what to expect. Upon arrival, they found no Germans, but no other Allied troops either.

They were the first liberation troops the Danes had seen. The Germans had retreated, leaving the Danes to fend for themselves. Fryklund and his RAF friend were stopped every few feet as they walked into Copenhagen by grateful, cheering Danes, asked for their autographs and invited to impromptu parties. Unfortunately for the RAF pilot, he had official duties to perform and set off for the dairy farms and fields of the country, but Fryklund recalls several days partying with the Danes. The only specific comment he would make about this time was 'Wartime liberation was never so much fun!'

First Sergeant Thomas Luke had a difficult time keeping the enlisted men occupied during the post-war months. Daily roll calls, camp duties and technical trades took up some of their time, but with no real urgency any more; what was the point? The squadron fielded several baseball teams to pass the time, even doing well in tournaments. Luke himself managed a week's leave in Switzerland, time he recalls fondly to this day.

Finally, a system for bringing troops home emerged. A 'points' system was developed; for each month a man had been overseas, he was awarded so many points. Likewise for each battle campaign, combat ribbon and the like. Those with points totalling over eighty should have been the first to go home, but naturally, it did not work out that way.

With the fighting still raging in Japan, the Air Force decided to send those newly arrived men, fresh from their technical training schools, home for thirty days' leave before shipping them to the Pacific to take part in the final campaigns. Since the new men did not really start going home until late June and July, and the Pacific War ended on 15 August 1945, the Air Force decided to discharge immediately those who were already in the United States.

From the financial and logistical standpoints, the decision made sense. To the long-serving, long-suffering men in the 417th, it stank. But, as always, they made the best of it.

In the days immediately following the ceasefire, the 417th moved several times. From Gebelstadt, they proceeded to Biblis (designated Y-78), then to Klein Genau near Darmstadt (Y-72). They flew from a grass strip covered by steel mesh plates – cheap to build, but more slippery than grease after it had rained. Bob Condon slid off the end of the runway after one such shower. So deep into the mud was his P-61 that the line crews had to use a small bulldozer called a cletrac to pull him free.

Unfortunately, even though the fighting was over, there was still some dying. As we saw in Chapter 1, Captain 'Duff' Campbell died in mid-May, only a week and a half after the fighting stopped.

Technical specialists for each of the Allied air forces scoured Germany for flyable examples of Nazi hardware. These scientists and engineers wanted to take the aircraft home to their respective countries so that they could be studied to make improvements in their own aeronautical industries. Some of the knowledge gained during this programme included swept-wing technology for jet aircraft, missile expertise for giant rockets and small anti-aircraft weapons.

The dirty work of finding such aircraft was farmed out to many units, one of them being the 417th. At an airfield outside Pilsen, Czechoslovakia, amid the smashed remains of a former German air base, rested several Me-109s still in good shape. The field was only about 2,000ft long and getting in a P-61, which was now used as a transport, was a challenge. On one of those challenges, the pilot smoked the brakes so much trying not to run off the runway that the brake drum fused to the wheel. Try as they might with the tools they had with them, the mechanics were unable to break it loose. They decided to leave the aircraft there and return the next day with a complete wheel assembly.

The next day, they loaded a P-61 wheel in the R/O's compartment in the extreme aft end of the Widow. The pilot, 'Ha Ha' Hoffman gunned the engines and the fighter-turned-cargo-plane leaped from the runway. As it did, the rest of the squadron was treated to the sight of a complete P-61 wheel careening down the runway. Not being strapped down in the R/O's compartment, it had shattered the plexiglass cone as the take-off acceleration forces slammed it backwards. Hoffman, unaware of his runaway cargo, had switched radio frequencies before the squadron could contact him. He got all the way to Pilsen and had to come back again for the spare wheel.

Using a captured German mechanic and several of the engineers from the squadron, one of the fighters was brought back to life. Such was the 109's reputation as a handling challenge (of more than 30,000 produced throughout the war, German records indicate that thousands were lost to handling accidents and not combat!), that the only pilot willing to attempt the flight was 'Duff' Campbell. He had no flight manual to help him and had to work out for himself where the various switches, gauges, and indicators were. Finally, in the late afternoon of 18 May 1945, he fired up the 109's Daimler-Benz inverted V in-line engine. After a few more minutes adjusting throttle friction, control surface movements and the like, he was ready. With a generous amount of rudder to keep the fighter on the runway, he clawed his way aloft.

Bob Condon, who was on hand to see the flight, says:

> In German ready-rooms at every fighter base, they had cautionary notes about the torque of the engine of these planes. It took full rudder to counteract it. We decided that Campbell must have used something less than full rudder, because as soon as the Me-109 cleared the ground, it went into a hard left-hand turn, and never straightened out. It went around 270 degrees and then the wingtip touched the ground and it rolled up in a ball and burned.

Crew chief and flight engineer Paul Peyron was one of the mechanics who had helped coax the German fighter to life. He too watched the tragic scene. 'We rushed over to the crash, but he made no attempt to evacuate the aircraft and we couldn't get to it. He burned up in the airplane.'

Following this accident only specialized technical units using test pilots and captured German fliers were allowed to salvage any German aircraft.

Unofficially, however, the young, bored pilots of the 417th

found themselves with plenty of hardware with which to get into trouble. At various times in the next few months the squadron had a German Bucker Bu-181 two-place trainer, a Grunau Baby 2 training glider, a Fiesler Storch short-take-off and -landing aircraft, a Seibel Si 204D liaison aircraft (a fairly large twin-engined aircraft), and even a couple of American aircraft, a Piper L-4 Cub and a Noorduyn UC-64 Norseman.

Bob Condon logged time in each of these, not content with risking his life in just the P-61. Regarding the docile Bu-181, he says:

> It was interesting trying to figure out how high and how fast I was using the metric dials on the instruments.
>
> The 181 was grounded after some GIs passing through cut off the swastikas on the tail for souvenirs. Since the tail was fabric, they just used a bayonet to rip them off. That was the end of that aircraft.

Of the glider Condon says:

> It was a 'primary' glider, which means the body was open framework and the pilot sat out front with nothing around him, and no instruments. We would tow it from a jeep using a 100ft rope which would get it up to about 50ft high. Then we'd cut loose and glide to a skidding halt in the tall grass.
>
> Few of the pilots would fly it. Too scary with no instruments, especially no air speed indicator. But they thought nothing of taking up a 4,000-hp brute full of 100 octane gasoline. Those of us who did fly it had a lot of fun until a landing hit a big rock tossed out of a bomb crater and busted the landing skid. It was made of laminated and glued wood and we had no way of fixing it.

His Fiesler flight was not supposed to be. The Storch's aileron and elevator cables had been disconnected and thus the aircraft was unflyable. It had been abandoned by the retreating Germans at the far end of the taxiway. Condon decided to taxi it closer so that he could work on it with the idea of getting it airborne eventually. 'I was fast idling along back down the taxi strip using the brakes and rudder when I noticed the ground receding from under me. The plane was 25ft up in the air!'

The Storch, an ugly, ungainly-looking aircraft, was renowned for its short take-off ability. For example, earlier in the war, after Italy had surrendered to the Allies, Benito Mussolini had been captured and imprisoned in a chalet on top of a mountain in the Italian Alps. His guards believed that any rescue attempt would come from the road, since the yard around the place was too tiny for any aircraft to land in, much less take off. In an amazing feat of derring-do, however, the famed German commando Otto Skorzeny landed with a small team of glider-borne troops, over-powered the dictator's guard and waited for his ride home. Soon a Storch, angular and awkward, alighted on the tiny area, took Mussolini and Skorzeny aboard, and leaped off the mountain top. Short take-off indeed!

Thus it should have come as no surprise to Condon that even a fast taxi would provide enough lift for his damaged Storch to fly. Thinking quickly, he pulled the throttle back and the plane gently eased back down. He took it to the new parking spot at a crawl. Unfortunately for him, the squadron moved again before he could repair it.

Condon even had adventures in the Piper Cub the squadron had somehow acquired. He was up one afternoon practising stalls, when the engine cut as he pulled the stick into his stomach, trying to make the docile little plane depart controlled flight. It was not a particularly dangerous thing to do, provided one had enough altitude to recover; the stall and recovery are among the more basic pilot manoeuvres.

On this occasion, however, the engine stopped. Since he was at 3,000ft, he had plenty of height to recover, so he dived and attempted to restart the engine. With no response from the little 60-hp four-cylinder engine, he looked for a place to land. He says:

The only suitable (almost) spot was a small, narrow ploughed field with a peach tree in the middle. I slipped it in to fence-top level, slid past the tree going sideways, straightened out, jammed it down, bounced once in the soft dirt, and hit three-point [on all three landing gear] 50ft later with the brakes locked. We skidded 25ft in the wet dirt and stopped.

Another tragedy struck on 28 June. Second Lieutenant Frank Cooley and his R/O, Lieutenant Gaines, were killed in a P-61 when the port engine pumped out gallons of oil and began smoking badly. Because of low clouds, he was flying along at less than 1,000ft. A relatively new pilot, he accidentally feathered the starboard engine and the aircraft dropped, hitting the ground so violently that wreckage was spewed for hundreds of feet in the resulting explosion.

Pilot Jim Van Voorhis says that in the early post-war months, the squadron, like hundreds of other flying units in Europe, had to fly once or twice a week in demonstrations of strength over Germany. These flights were reminders to the German nation that it was well and truly conquered. It also kept the units busy while the 'brass' decided when and how to send the men home.

The squadron also maintained alert aircraft to cover any eventuality and even scrambled one night in late July against an in-bound 'bogey'. It turned out to be an RAF Lancaster heavy bomber, off course with radio failure, but for a while the old adrenalin came rushing back to the troops.

As the other night-fighter squadrons closed, the 417th was officially designated as part of the army of occupation. Besides the flights and station moves, the squadron kept busy trying to cope with the literally hundreds of personnel shifts. As other units were deactivated, some of their men would be attached to the 417th for administrative purposes while they waited for their ticket back home. The 417th's official history is full of entries showing men being assigned to the squadron, then only days later being detached for their homeward journeys.

In the pell-mell rush to demobilize, hundreds of magnificent aircraft that had been designed to fight no longer had a purpose. Many of them flew into Darmstadt and were abandoned. So numerous were the P-61s received from other night-fighter squadrons like the 422nd, 423rd and 414th, that they were blown up and bulldozed into pits to make room for yet more arrivals – a sad fate for such proud warriors.

Finally, in late August and early September, the 417th's old hands had their chance to go home. Technical Sergeant Paul Peyron, a crew chief from the beginning back in Florida, began his trip on 6 September, enduring open box cars to a holding camp, the famous Camp Lucky Strike east of Paris, then on to Marseilles for a troopship to New York. He was demobbed in October.

By the end of September, the 417th had lost nearly all of its original personnel and only gained a few dozen replacements. The squadron roster for the 1 October 1945 report contains only sixty-four names, from a normal complement of over 200! German prisoners and the numerous displaced persons left scattered in the aftermath of the war were pressed into service to run various areas like the switchboard, the mess hall, etc. By the end of the year, however, the squadron began receiving more replacements so that it became more of a regular unit again.

CHAPTER 13

As Peyron and others left, their places were taken by a fresh crop of airmen. Three of them, Terry Carter, Rich Ziebart, and John Roberson, all shared the disappointment of being just too late to get to flying school. By mid-1944, the US Army Air Forces realized that it would have enough aviators to finish the war and drastically reduced the size of its training pipeline. Men like Carter, Ziebart and Roberson, too young to join up earlier, had enlisted in various programmes like the aviation cadets, waiting for the chance to finish training and qualify for flying.

Instead they were shuttled into enlisted specialities which did not involve handling the controls of an aircraft. Carter found himself going through B-29 gunnery schools in Denver and Las Vegas; Ziebart became a radio operator/radio maintenance specialist; Roberson found himself, by his own admission, staring quizzically at the inner workings of the B-29s intricate Wright R-3350 engines after being sent to engine mechanic training.

Terry Carter recalls his disappointment at not becoming a pilot, but then relates an incident that turned him off flying.

My crew was sent to Chatham Field, Georgia for crew training in July 1945. On one training mission, our flight engineer, who was actually a surplus pilot, left the oil cooler flaps closed on take-off. The B-29 had a reputation for catastrophic engine failures, most due to overheating. On a hot July day in Georgia, this guy's negligence, or maybe just inadequate training, nearly killed us.

I was in the waist section along with three other gunners. In the forward – or nose section were five officers – pilot, co-pilot, bombardier, navigator and flight engineer – and one enlisted man, the radio operator.

It soon became obvious that we weren't gaining any altitude or airspeed and were barely above the treetops over Georgia swampland. We were about 8 miles from the airfield when the pilot did a 180-degree turn and headed back to Chatham.

It was an agonizing, terror-filled few minutes. To crash in that swampland would have meant instant, fiery death. But our pilots managed to get the aircraft back to the edge of the runway, whereupon it lurched violently to starboard, shearing off the right wing, clean with the fuselage, and immediately burst into flames.

Miraculously, the momentum carried the rest of the plane beyond the flames and our entire crew escaped with nary a scratch. But fear of flying in B-29s had been embedded in us to varying degrees. Nevertheless, our training continued.

Then came the fateful day in August 1945. We were relaxing in the dayroom when word came that a single, incredibly powerful bomb had obliterated the Japanese city of Hiroshima. The war was soon over and B-29 gunners were no longer needed.

Instead, I got shipped to Germany as a P-61 turret technician, working on the top turret that held four .50 caliber machine guns on some of the Widow models.

Rich Ziebart arrived in Germany in the bitter cold of January 1946. Reporting to the 417th, then at Rothwestern Airfield near Kassel under the command of Captain Ted Deakyne, with two other radio men. Deakyne told them he needed a radar man and Ziebart drew the duty.

There was not much difference in repairing radar sets or radio sets as the components were much the same. The secret was knowing how it worked. I have to admit that there was not a day that I felt I didn't want to learn more. Vacuum tubes had the very same problems in both radio and radar sets, so if you understood the make-up of the tubes, you usually could fix the problems.

On one occasion I was to demonstrate how the SCR-720 radar scope worked at a review. During this review the set I was showing would not operate so unless I could clear the scope to show clear grid lines it was useless. We had a remedy for this by picking up the front of the set ½ in and letting it drop; the vacuum tube that was causing the problem would correct itself.

Well, this did not impress the colonel who was viewing my demonstration and he very politely told me I was being careless with our secret radar even though the set corrected itself in front of him.

I felt bad, but I knew I could not explain why it was necessary to do what I did.

Ziebart was also in on the beginnings of the Cold War.

Rothwesten Airfield was on the border of the line separating the Russian Zone from the American Zone so we always saw the Soviet soldiers marching along the airstrip. We had to protect our P-61s day and night to keep the Russians from entering our area and stealing the radar.

We finally moved the squadron to Fitzlar Airfield, a little further away, to keep the Russians away from our airplanes.

Ziebart got his first taste of flying in the Widow when he badgered one of the squadron pilots to take him up so he could operate the radar in the air. On the day of the flight, however, the pilot changed the plan. Handing Ziebart a bucket, he made him sit in the gunner's seat, which was behind and higher than the cockpit. Another pilot in a second P-61 flew alongside Ziebart's aircraft, and the two tried to outdo the other in hair-raising flying. Ziebart recalls:

When the pilot handed me the pail, he said, 'Here, you are going to need this and don't miss or you are going to clean up the airplane.'

The maneuvers consisted of seeing how fast you could climb and then how fast you could dive straight down again. I do remember coming over a river and flying over a hay field where some poor farmer had just loaded a wagon full of hay. There was no hay left after both planes went just above him.

The spaghetti I had for lunch was also all in the pail, and

none on the plane. I only wish I knew who that pilot was. I would thank him today for the only time I was up in the 'Wild Blue Yonder' during my Air Corps career.

John Roberson was another would-be pilot that the war passed by. When his turn finally came to enter the Air Force, B-29 engine mechanics were in demand. After he had trained on the intricate 18-cylinder R-3350 compound engine, the Pacific War ended and Roberson found himself with orders to the army of occupation in Germany. Like Ziebart, he arrived in the winter of 1946, enduring several bone-numbing days in an open box car travelling from Camp Lucky Strike to the 417th at Kassel.

> I was assigned at first as an assistant crew chief to a P-61. It was kind of a 'monkey see, monkey do' arrangement. I would watch, assist, and learn from the crew chief and try to pick up those skills.
>
> It was cold during February when I arrived. We had to do most of our work on the airplanes outside. For cold-weather gear we wore the fleece-lined, fake-leather outer garments that bomber gunners wore to protect them from the sub-zero temperatures at altitude. Only those garments were actually made of oil-impregnated thick paper with a sprayed-on lining not of wool but some sort of paper as well. It was bulky gear and many times, to reach our hands inside the engine nacelles, we had to remove the garment, sometimes even our jacket and shirt to snake our hands in.
>
> Invariably, you'd work on something like a fuel pump or the like, with your hands above your head and gas would run down the length of your arm, pooling in your armpit. And it was cold!

It was so cold, that Roberson, with a temperature of 105 degrees, found himself hospitalized with pneumonia for nearly two months. Discharged at the end of April, he rejoined the 417th at its base at Fitzlar, where he was promoted to corporal just in time to help with another unit move, this time to Schweinfurt. He also advanced to being a crew chief himself, having his very own P-61 to care for.

He says of his post-war time overseas, 'Germany was a nice

place, particularly the parts largely untouched by the war. Schweinfurt and Kassel, however, were just the opposite, nothing really but cities of rubble. It was interesting to me to see the Germans sift through a ruined city and salvage everything they could to rebuild it.'

As 1946 progressed, the 417th's time stretched into liberal leaves all around Europe, casual flying, taking classes, and generally killing time as part of the US Army of Occupation. Men continued to flow in and out of the squadron as the military contracted to a fraction of its wartime size. But from its nearly total depletion at the end of 1945, the squadron became one of the largest in the world. For example, upon the deactivation of the 36th Fighter Group, all of its personnel were transferred to the 417th. Instead of a couple of hundred men, over a thousand could now claim the 417th as home. The squadron size constantly expanded and contracted as the military reorganized itself, but it muddled along, flying only occasionally now.

The last commander of the squadron before its deactivation, Major John M. Konosky, took over from Ted Deakyne, who finally went home after more than five years of combat in the RCAF and USAAF. Konosky did much to raise the morale of the 417th during his tenure. Better food, more flying, and attention to military duties reflected his sense of discipline. He also hosted General Carl 'Tooey' Spaatz, long the commander of all US Army Air Forces in Europe during an inspection tour in July.

Finally and unexpectedly, towards the end of the year, it was all over. The 417th Night-fighter Squadron was deactivated on 6 November 1946.

In the years since World War II, the squadron has been reactivated and deactivated several more times. Its first post-war appearance was as the 417th Fighter-Bomber Squadron (FBS) at Clovis Air Force Base (AFB), New Mexico, on 1 January 1953, flying North American F-51 Mustangs. It soon moved again to Germany, where it was equipped with the North American F-86 Sabre jet fighter.

Among its commanding officers in Germany, two are of particular note. One was Lieutenant Colonel 'Dick' McCray who had previously flown in and eventually commanded the squadron during the war. The other is the world famous pilot, then a major,

Charles 'Chuck' Yeager.

In 1958, the squadron traded in its F-86s for the North American F-100 Super Sabre, which it flew for the next ten years. Then the massive McDonnell-Douglas F-4 Phantom II became standard equipment and the unit moved back to New Mexico, but this time to Holloman AFB as part of the 49 Tactical Fighter Wing (TFW).

In 1972, the 417th again became involved in a shooting war with its deployment to Takhli, Thailand before returning back to Holloman. It was deactivated in 1977.

Then the squadron was secretly reactivated at Tonopah Test Range, Nevada, as one of the original stealth squadrons, flying the Lockheed F-117 Nighthawk. Now known as the Bandits, the squadron flew combat missions in Operation Desert Storm before moving from the secrecy of the Nevada desert to Holloman AFB once again.

The 417th was deactivated again on 2 December 1993 as the United States Air Force (USAF) reorganized the naming of its flying squadrons. It stood down for perhaps the last time and was renumbered as the 7th Fighter Squadron. At the time of writing, the 417th is carried on the USAF's inactive roles, waiting again for its call to colours should it be needed.

EPILOGUE

They are mostly all gone now. Time has done what enemy action could not. Most of them are not mentioned in this book, either because they have passed away or because I have been unable to contact them or their families. A very few did not want to discuss the subject and I respect their wishes.

But just because they are not included does not diminish their importance and their contributions to the squadron. Like most servicemen and women, their efforts are largely unsung but vital to getting the mission accomplished. The roster of personnel changed regularly, as does any unit's. With each changing of the names, the squadron's personality also changed just a bit.

Fighting the enemy and, at times, their own aircraft and supply system, they did their duty, no matter what. They were not the most famous and they did not shoot down the most aircraft. But like most Americans in every conflict, they did what was required of them to accomplish the mission – not for glory, not for headlines, but for each other. Crew chiefs and radar technicians put in the long hours because they did not want to be the ones who let a crew down. Crews flew the ragged, rugged Beaufighter in all kinds of weather, covering their patrol areas because they did not want the ports, ships and troops counting on the night fighter's protection to be attacked. This is their legacy and one that can still be seen in today's airmen as they fly in conflicts in distant places.

Those that came home, however, put the war behind them and helped build America into the most prosperous, most powerful nation in the world. They did that task like they did their wartime duty, without a lot of fanfare, without a lot of drama, and mostly in their own small ways.

The thinning ranks of the 417th include a fair number of doctors, lawyers, electronics executives, businessmen and technical craftsmen. After the war, not a few remained in the service and went on to a full military career. Some left and were recalled during the Korean War, serving their nation once again.

No matter what their fates after the war, the vast majority of the squadron were touched by their experiences in Florida, England, Africa, France and Germany.

They stayed in contact with each other through the squadron's association and through many reunions through the years.

It seems an essential part of them and who they became. Shaped by the biggest event in human history, they made it a part of themselves for ever. For example, Andrew Bernard, one of the original group to be shipped out in 1943, as a corporal, died in 1968. Except for his dates of birth and death, the only inscription on his tombstone reads '417th Night Fighter Squadron.' Not a bad way to be remembered.

APPENDIX I

The Overseas Movement Roster of the 417th NFS

The following is taken from GHQ AAF SO (General Headquarters, Army Air Forces Special Order) 114, dated 24 April 1943. It is the final roster of the 417th prior to boarding transport for overseas duty.

NAME	RANK	FUNCTION
JOSEPH T. EHLINGER	CAPT	COMDG O
JOSEPH H. DOUGHERTY	CAPT	INTELL O
ARTHUR J. KATZBERG	1ST LT	FLT SURGEON
GEORGE E. NELSON	1ST LT	RADIO (S)
SUBHI M. SADI	1ST LT	INTELL O
ROWAN A. WILLIAMS	1ST LT	SUPPLY O
J. D. (IO) BROWN	2ND LT	ADJ
KENNETH (NMI) CAMPBELL	2ND LT	ENG O
HERMAN C. DOESCHER	2ND LT	ARMAMENT
CARLETON B. FRAZEE	2ND LT	WEATHER O
WALTER G. GROOM	2ND LT	PILOT
SAMUEL B. HOOTON	2ND LT	PILOT
GEORGE D. HUGHES	2ND LT	PILOT
JOHN F. KIRWIN	2ND LT	PILOT
WILLIAM A. LARSEN	2ND LT	PILOT
JOHN S. M. LEE*	2ND LT	PILOT
JOSEPH E. LEONARD*	2ND LT	PILOT
WILLIAM J. LODGE JR	2ND LT	STATISTICAL O
ALEXANDER L. MACQUEEN JR*	2ND LT	PILOT
CLARENCE R. MCCRAY	2ND LT	PILOT
HUMPHREY M. MALLORY	2ND LT	PILOT
GEORGE A. MOESER	2ND LT	ORDINANCE O
JAMES J. SIMPSON	2ND LT	UNKNOWN
HERMAN A. STIRNUS	2ND LT	PILOT
CHESTER E. WATSON*	2ND LT	PILOT
CLARENCE K. FULLER*	F/O	PILOT

RAYFORD W. JEFFREY	F/O	PILOT
ROLAND O. LEEMAN	F/O	PILOT
FRANK (NMI) MCLAIN*	F/O	PILOT
WILLIAM R. WILLIAMSON	F/O	PILOT
ALPHEUS L. WITHERS	1ST LT	GCI O
MAURICE J. LONG	2ND LT	GCI O
HARRY A. PALMER	2ND LT	GCI O
WILLIAM WHEELER III	2ND LT	GCI O
CHARLES F. HOCKMAN	1ST SGT	
AUDREY M. CHRISTENSEN	M/SGT	
KENNETH W MIDDOUR	M/SGT	
EUGENE O. MOORE	M/SGT	
ROBERT A. PERRY	M/SGT	
ELZA (NMI) SWAIN JR	M/SGT	
EARL A. WETHERALD	M/SGT	
ROBERT L. BECK	T/SGT	
JENNINGS B. BLANKENSHIP JR	T/SGT	
PAT D. CARL	T/SGT	
ABBOT J. COOK	T/SGT	
JOSEPH (NMI) GONZALES	T/SGT	
ROY E. HEDRICK	T/SGT	
WAYNE H. MCMINIMENT	T/SGT	
RICHARD C. MOSER	T/SGT	
OSCAR P. RICE	T/SGT	
GEORGE W. ROBINSON	T/SGT	
PHIL P. SARTIN	T/SGT	
ROBERT G. THOMPSON	T/SGT	
JOHN (NMI) ZAPANTIS	T/SGT	
RAYMOND CHRISTENSEN*	S/SGT	
ROY W. HALL	S/SGT	
WILLIAM A. HENDERSON	S/SGT	
HARRY D. HERBERT	S/SGT	
RICHARD J. HOVERSON	S/SGT	
EDWARD W. HURTA	S/SGT	
LORENZO R. PETERS	S/SGT	
ALLEN A. SAMSON	S/SGT	
JOHN J. SOBCZAK	S/SGT	
WILLIAM A. ANDERSON	SGT	
MURREL W. ANDERTON JR*	SGT	
ORVILLE A. ARENDS	SGT	
MINOR R. ATKINSON	SGT	
ORVILLE W. BAKER	SGT	
GEORGE W. BAUMGARDNER	SGT	
EARLEY R. BASS	SGT	
LESTER E. BEENE	SGT	
JOSEPH H. BELL	SGT	
SHERMAN (NMI) BOYD	SGT	
RUDOLPH B. BROWN	SGT	
STANLEY E. CHMIELEWSKE	SGT	
JAMES D. CLARK	SGT	

FREDRICK J. COLVILLE	SGT
MILTON B. CROSS JR	SGT
MATTHEW F. FILIPOWICZ	SGT
JAMES M. FINNERTY	SGT
IRVIN E. GATHRIGHT	SGT
GEORGE L. HASSLER	SGT
DAVID G. IVES	SGT
JAMES G. KEANE	SGT
AFTON (NMI) KOSICK	SGT
BRUCE B. MCGHIE	SGT
JAMES J. MCINTYRE	SGT
CORNELIUS J. MCNULTY	SGT
LEWIS A. MILLER	SGT
RICHARD O. NEEL	SGT
STEPHEN E. PEERY JR	SGT
PAUL C. PEYRON	SGT
FREDERICK O. POND	SGT
CARROLL F. POOLE	SGT
WALTER J. PRESTON	SGT
NICHOLAS C. RAPUANO	SGT
ARTHUR (NMI) REED	SGT
SAMUEL (NMI) RESNICK	SGT
WALLACE G. RODLAND	SGT
PHILIP (NMI) ROSSMAN	SGT
AARON G. STEINER	SGT
HARRY W. TUCKER*	SGT
LINDSAY J. WILLEY	SGT
MARTIN W. ZENGE	SGT
EDWARD T. AKIKIE	CPL
FELIX A. ARANOWSKI	CPL
ELLERY C. BADGERO	CPL
DONALD E. BAKER	CPL
REUBEN (NMI) BALLOW	CPL
WARREN L. BARNEY JR	CPL
IRVING W. BASSOW	CPL
ALBERT R. BATTISTONI	CPL
JOHN F. BAUBLIS	CPL
ROBERT N. BAUER	CPL
BONNIE L. BENEFIELD*	CPL
ANDREW BERNARD	CPL
WILLIAM A. BERNSTEIN	CPL
ISAAC (NMI) BETON	CPL
ALBERT S. BETTENCOURT	CPL
ROBERT L. BOSSHART	CPL
MICHAEL (NMI) BRECHUN	CPL
ROBERT J. BRENNAN	CPL
CHARLES E. BRIGDEN	CPL
SAMUEL O. BRILES	CPL
LEO C. BRODIE	CPL
LEO R. BROWN	CPL

DONALD H. BURRIER	CPL
ANGELO J. CERVO	CPL
JACK (NMI) CHOOLJIAN	CPL
GEORGE E. CROUCH	CPL
ROBERT L. CULP	CPL
ROBERT J. DAVIS	CPL
MICHAEL (NMI) DEMEDA	CPL
TELLO (NMI) DE SANTIS*	CPL
RICHARD (NMI) DONOVAN	CPL
JOE F. DRAPER	CPL
WALTER T. DYER JR*	CPL
DAROLD H. ENGLEHARDT	CPL
CHARLES W. FAHRBACK	CPL
JOHN J. F. FENIMORE	CPL
ASHLEY S. FOSTER	CPL
JAMES F. GENESSE JR	CPL
MAURICE J. GILLICK	CPL
RAYMOND J. GOERES	CPL
IRVING I. GOLD	CPL
STEPHEN T. GRACHEN	CPL
CLODIO (NMI) GRAPPONE	CPL
ERNEST A. GRIFFITH*	CPL
EDWARD G. HAFF	CPL
BASIL D. HALL	CPL
RALPH B. HANNA JR	CPL
JOSEPH J. HENDERSCHOTT	CPL
BERTRAM (NMI) HOLLAND JR	CPL
RUDOLH J. HODUL	CPL
ROBERT M. HUTCHISON JR	CPL
CLARENCE W. JENSEN	CPL
HAROLD A. JOHNSON JR	CPL
RALPH H. JONES	CPL
BURTON B. KNOPP	CPL
ABRAHAM (NMI) KAPLON	CPL
RALPH H. KOSKI JR	CPL
HENRY F. KONTER	CPL
REGIS W. LANDY	CPL
ROLAND D. LAWYER	CPL
BARON H. LEVY	CPL
WILLIAM J. LINDSEY	CPL
ALBERT (NMI) LIPKIN	CPL
EDWARD J. MAHON	CPL
ASHER (NMI) MEDVID	CPL
DAVID (NMI) MILLER	CPL
JAKE D. MILLER	CPL
LYLE J. MOMTBRIAND	CPL
MARTIN T. MOODY JR	CPL
CLIFFORD H. MORTON	CPL
JOHN R. MUSICARO	CPL
DONALD R. OLSEN	CPL

EDWARD J. O'NEILL	CPL
JAMES S. PACKARD	CPL
JOHN (NMI) PAVLIK	CPL
CHARLES F. POEKERT	CPL
PAUL R. PROCTOR	CPL
ANTONIO (NMI) PUENTE	CPL
JAMES T. QUINTY	CPL
MARX B. RASBACK	CPL
EPHRAM M. RIDGEWAY	CPL
GEORGE M. ROBINSON	CPL
WALTER J. RUNOWSKI	CPL
JOHN W. SCHMITT	CPL
PHILIP M. SHERR	CPL
MATHEW T SMITH	CPL
ELLSWORTH J. SNOW	CPL
GERALD F. STOECKEL	CPL
WILLIAM A. STUERZEL	CPL
HORACE W. TATUM	CPL
CHARLES R. TOMPHINS	CPL
FRANK J TRACY	CPL
JOSEPH M. VAN LAECKEN	CPL
JAMES R. VAN VALKENBURGH	CPL
MELVIN A. VERSTOPPEN	CPL
ROBERT E. WASHINGER	CPL
MURRAY (NMI) WAYNE	CPL
HALTER H. WILKE	CPL
ROBERT J. WITTWER	CPL
ARTHUR (NMI) WRAY	CPL
MATTHEW V. ZAJONC	CPL
LEO (NMI) ZUCKERMAN	CPL
THOMAS W. ANDREWS	PFC
ORAN R. BALDWIN	PFC
CARROLL A. BLACK	PFC
HARRY E. COSPER	PFC
CARROLL A. BLACK	PFC
THOMAS N. CRANDALL	PFC
MAX (NMI) DONNER	PFC
WILLIAM F. ERNST JR	PFC
WOODROW (NMI) HALSEY	PFC
CHARLES G. HANCOCK	PFC
JAMES T. HARRAH	PFC
THOMAS HASTINGS	PFC
HARRY E. HIBNER JR	PFC
JESSE L. JAMESON	PFC
HARRIS D. REYNOLDS	PFC
JOSEPH S. SOUZA	PFC
MEYER (NMI) STOLLER	PFC
JOHN W. SWAIM	PFC
CLARENCE F. BARRY	PVT
JAMES (NMI) BELCASTRO	PVT

KENNETH C. BLOCKSOM	PVT
EARL S. BRYAN	PVT
ADEN H. CAMERON	PVT
JACK T. CHRISTENSEN	PVT
JOHN F. CLEMMENS	PVT
HARLEN G. COLEMAN JR	PVT
SALVATORE (NMI) CONSIGLEO	PVT
DAN B. CORDELL	PVT
RANDALL W. COTTRELL	PVT
JIMMIE (NMI) CURNUTT	PVT
ADAMS B. DARRELL	PVT
GEORGE E. DELLINGER	PVT
JOSEPH J. DI CAPRIO	PVT
HESSEL (NMI) DYKSTRA	PVT
CHARLES A. ENGLAND	PVT
THOMAS A. FRAMBES	PVT
ABRAHAM H. GARMISE	PVT
PETER C. GOPSHES	PVT
BENJAMIN (NMI) GURA	PVT
EMANUEL (NMI) HALCOMB	PVT
MARVIN (NMI) HALL	PVT
ROBERT D. HAMILTON	PVT
JOHN E. HEANEY	PVT
EARL F. HISSETT	PVT
HAROLD W. HOFFMAN	PVT
THOMAS D. HUFFMAN	PVT
SAMUEL L. HUGHEY	PVT
HOWARD A. KOHRMAN*	PVT
EDWARD F. LENARD	PVT
ALBERT L. LEWIS	PVT
HOWARD S. MCCAIN	PVT
ROBERT F. MCKENZIE	PVT
FRANK J. MULLEN	PVT
MARSHALL J. NEWTON	PVT
WILLIAM E. OEHRTMAN	PVT
LEONARD R. POTTER*	PVT
GERALD E. CHRISTINE	PVT
HAROLD L. ROTH	PVT
JOHN F. SHANNON	PVT
ANTHONY A. SPEIER JR	PVT
CECIL L. TAYLOR	PVT
SA C. TRIMBOLI	PVT
DAVID T. TUTTLE	PVT
NEAL D. WILLIS	PVT
CHARLES M. YERICO	PVT

*Killed while assigned to 417th NFS. The squadron lost thirty-one men during its World War II and occupation service. The breakdown of casualties is as follows:

Pilots	14, 10 in Beaufighters, 2 in P-61s, 1 in Me-109, 1 murdered
R/Os	10, 9 in Beaufighters, 1 in P-61
Crew chiefs	2, both in Beaufighters
Cooks	3, 2 in vehicle accident, 1 of illness
Others	2, both in vehicle accident.

APPENDIX II

The Bristol Beaufighter

The Bristol Beaufighter was everything it was designed to be and more. Blunt, tenacious, versatile, it would perform more types of mission than its designers ever imagined. Conceived at the outset of the Second World War, it was still soldiering on long into the jet age.

In 1938, the Bristol Aircraft Company submitted a proposal to meet the RAF's need for a cannon-armed fighter. In the rush to rearm before the war, the RAF saw that cannons were needed to knock down the new breed of bombers that Germany was fielding. Bristol proposed a variation of its successful Beaufort torpedo bomber as just the thing the RAF needed.

Bristol originally envisaged using most of the main components of the Beaufort, thus saving both design and development costs. By using the same wings, rear fuselage and tail unit, they sought to use the same tooling jigs which were already producing the Beaufort. The RAF expressed reservations about the size of the proposed fighter; a twin-engined two-seater was thought to be rather large for a fighter, but since Bristol planned to put in at least four 20mm cannon they gave the go-ahead for production in 1939.

As the design progressed from proposal to construction, the need for many changes became obvious. For example, the decision to use the more powerful Hercules VI radial engine rather than the Hercules II originally suggested necessitated a larger propeller. To ensure proper ground clearance for them, the engine nacelles were moved from underneath the wing to a mid-wing mount. The repositioned nacelles required the gear oleo legs be lengthened.

Even though the RAF was primarily interested in getting a cannon-armed fighter into squadron service in the shortest time possible, a secondary armament of eight .303 Browning machine-guns was always considered a necessity. The machine-guns could add additional firepower when going against bombers, but could also be useful for ground attacks against troops, where the punch of the 20mm guns was not as effective as the ability to spray lots of lead over a large area.

Originally, Bristol planned to put the eight guns in a protruding belly blister. The Air Ministry thought this protuberance would add to drag and slow down the big fighter. Instead, they asked Bristol to place the machine-guns in the wings. Bristol, however, protested that they were well into the construction of the prototype. Incorporating four machine-guns in the port wing would mean a delay since the gun placement meant repositioning the large landing light. Instead, they asked to place only two guns in this wing and four in the starboard wing. In order to keep development on track, the Air Ministry agreed, so the Beaufighter would pack a powerful if asymmetrical punch of four 20mm guns in the nose and six .303 machine-guns in the wings. This was the most powerful standard armament of any Allied fighter aircraft of the war.

All these changes substantially altered the original design proposal, with the result that very few parts of the Beaufort were interchangeable with the new fighter. It therefore acquired its own name, the Beaufighter, in May 1939.

After the prototype first flew in October 1939, the RAF's concerns about the feasibility of a big twin-engined aircraft successfully competing in the fighter arena increased. A maximum speed of 335mph at 16,800ft was short of the desired goal of 350mph. Although the Beaufighter handled reasonably well according to Bristol's chief test pilot, C.F. Uwins, it suffered from longitudinal instability and was not manoeuvrable enough to serve as a day fighter. This instability was to plague the Beau throughout its career, giving it a reputation for being a handful during take-off and landing.

A 1940 Air Fighting Development Unit pilot report, says the Beaufighter

...was found to handle as described in the handbook, but the stall is not so vicious as stated. Nevertheless, there is a feeling that the aircraft is a heavily loaded one and care must be taken when near the ground to maintain full flying speed or the aircraft will drop out of your hands. The take-off is straight-forward, although there is a slight tendency for the aircraft to swing to starboard; this is easily corrected by use of the rudder.

As 1939 turned into 1940, the RAF realized that it was woefully unprepared for night fighting, particularly in defensive operations. Air Marshall Dowding and other RAF leaders realized that the magnificent Chain Home radar stations would play a crucial role in the forthcoming Battle of Britain. They also knew that if they were successful in preventing the Germans from attacking Britain during the day, then they would surely turn to night bombing, where the front-line Spitfires and Hurricanes would be nearly useless.

The rudimentary airborne radars then under development required a fairly large aircraft to accommodate the bulky equipment, aerials and additional operator. The Beaufighter was a fairly large aircraft in need of a new mission and thus was born a match, if not made in heaven, then certainly fortuitous.

During the first of several prototype-testing regimes, the RAF adapted the Beau as a night fighter and urged Bristol to speed both testing and production to equip newly formed front-line night-fighter squadrons.

By late autumn of 1940, the first Beaus, designated Mk IF, were flying night patrols. On the night of 19/20 November, a 604 Squadron Beaufighter piloted by Flight Lieutenant John Cunningham and R/O Sergeant John Phillipson achieved the first radar-assisted kill. This form of electronic warfare became known as airborne interception (AI).

The Beau would go on to be the primary night fighter for the RAF until the introduction of the de Havilland Mosquito in late 1943. Even after this came into service, however, the Beau soldiered on in its first combat role until nearly the end of the war.

Even while Bristol scrambled to fill the orders for Mk IF night fighters, the RAF realized that the Beau was a marvellous platform for a variety of other attack missions. Coastal Command, which was responsible for patrolling the sea lanes so vital for the very survival of Britain, became the next user. In the Mk IC model, its squadrons began patrolling the vast expanse of the Bay of Biscay, searching for German U-boats.

In addition to this role, Beaufighters were also pressed into service as fighters in Coastal Command. German Ju-88s were plentiful, seeking out Allied merchant convoys to bomb and strafe. Beaus were often the only protection a convoy had against a harassing enemy strike aircraft. The Beaus generally acquitted themselves well in these aerial combats.

As the war progressed, the Beaufighter's offensive capabilities were expanded. The striking power of the heavy armament was impressive, especially once rockets were added. These 60lb armour-piercing and high-explosive projectiles added a substantial punch. Devastatingly effective against both ground and maritime targets, the rockets inspired confidence in the crews and dread in the enemy. Also, by 1944, the Beau began carrying torpedoes to increase the damage it could inflict.

Following the war, most Beaufighters were either scrapped or turned into target tugs. A few soldiered on in smaller nations' air forces, but the vast majority faded away.

As I have said, the first models were the Mk IF night fighter and Mk IC Coastal Command strike aircraft. The Mk I can easily be distinguished by its flat tailplanes. These horizontal stabilizers, with 0 degree of incidence, contributed to the Beau's problems in the pitch axis. Much work went into trying to correct this fault.

The Mk II was a Merlin-engined version. From the start of production, Bristol and the RAF feared that the Hercules engines would not be available in sufficient numbers to equip all the new Beaufighter units, so the legendary Merlin of Spitfire, Hurricane, P-51 Mustang and Lancaster fame was adapted to the Beau's frame. In a rare instance of no design improvement, the Mk II had an even worse reputation for handling than the Hercules-powered versions. With powerful engines and large propellers providing thrust at the extreme front and the rest of the large aircraft trailing aft, the gyroscopic effect was tremendous and contributed greatly to the Beaus reputation for difficult handling. The MK II's Merlin nacelles were even longer than those of the radial Hercules so the handling was commensurately worse. The Mk IIs saw only limited front line service before being relegated to training roles.

The Mk III and Mk IV were proposed 'slim' fuselage developments but were never actually built. The Mk V was an aberration that assuaged the RAF's love affair with turrets on fighters. Like the earlier Boulton-Paul Defiant single-engined fighter, the single-turreted Beau was not successful and only two were built.

The Mk VI was the first to get most of the Beau's faults corrected. Most noticeable was the 12-degree dihedral of the tailplanes. This simple modification went a long way to minimize the pitch sensitivity of Bristol's big fighter. Many of the earlier Mk I and Mk IIs were retrofitted with the angled horizontal stabilizers. Later versions of the Mk VI had increased range but at the expense of firepower. Long-range tanks were fitted into the wing machine-gun bays. Using a cruise speed of 243mph, they had a range of 1,810 miles compared to 1,480 in earlier marks.

The Mk VII was a one-off turbo supercharged Hercules-powered version with four-bladed propellers. The Mk VIII and Mk IX were reserved for Australian production but the designations were never used. The Mk X Beaufighters at first differed from their siblings in having a more powerful Hercules XVII engine modified for low-altitude operations. In addition to carrying a torpedo or a 500lb bomb on the centre line, two 250lb bombs could be carried under the wings. Later Mk Xs had a dorsal fin extension fitted. This additional longitudinal structure helped improve the Beau's handling even more with larger weapons loads of 1,000lb bombs on each wing. The last Beaufighter, built on 21 September 1945, was a Mk X.

The Mk 21 was an Australian-built version and was essentially the same as the Mk X with the exception of a noticeable 'bump' on the nose that housed a Sperry autopilot.

Well over 5,000 Beaufighters were built from 1939 to 1945, with Australia producing 364 of those under licence. In addition to the RAF and the USAAF, Beaufighters served in the RCAF, the Royal New Zealand Air Force (RNZAF), the Royal Australian Air Force (RAAF), the Portuguese navy, and the armed forces of Turkey, Israel and the Dominican Republic.

Turkey acquired nine RAF machines during the war and

purchased an additional twenty-three in 1946. Very little is known of how the Turkish air force operated these machines, or for how long.

Ten Mk Xs saw service under Dominican Republic colours and saw action at least once. On 20 June 1949, flying in concert with Mosquitoes, some attacked a Guatemalan invasion force. The strike helped to repulse the invasion. The last Dominican Beaus were retired in 1954.

Four Beaufighter Mk Xs were smuggled into Israel in the summer of 1948. They took part in numerous ground-attack sorties, including one remarkable incident when ex-RAF pilot Len Fitchett out-manoeuvred an Egyptian Sea Fury single-engined fighter at low level. Fitchett's adroit handling of the Beau caused the Fury to stall while lining up for a shot, and it crashed into the Red Sea. Sadly, Fitchett was killed shortly afterwards while conducting another ground-attack mission. By November 1948, Israel's Beaus were no longer logistically maintainable and were struck off charge. In 1994, the remains of Fitchett's aircraft was discovered during construction work in southern Israel. The scattered bits and pieces are now on display at the IAF Museum at Hazterim, Israel.

The Portuguese navy received sixteen Mk Xs during March, 1945. They flew them on maritime patrol and long-range fighter missions. One crashed in October of that year, killing its pilot, First Lieutenant Felix Lobo and two other crew members. In 1946, Portugal bought a replacement, but by 1949, a lack of spares and qualified pilots grounded all their Beaus. One of them was given back to the RAF and is on display in the RAF Museum at Hendon. Another was exchanged with South Africa for a Spitfire for Portugal's air museum. The rest were scrapped.

American pilot George 'Ghost' Aubill recalls that the Beaufighter had 'wonderful visibility, everything was easy to see including the plate-sized marine compass. It was a lot of fun on the deck, but since it didn't have superchargers, it was underpowered at altitude.'

With three kills to his name, Dr Harold Augsperger, says the aircraft 'wouldn't stay trimmed up no matter what you did. You had to work the throttles and brakes carefully once the tail dropped on landing. Likewise, the rudder wasn't really effective until the tail came up, but once you were out of those situations, the Beau flew just fine. It wasn't heavy on any axis and had very good visibility.'

One Portuguese Naval pilot, Second Lieutenant Manuel Beja once had an engine pack up while on a long cross-country flight. The other engine was spewing oil at an alarming rate and the engine temperature rose drastically. Thinking he would not be able to make it back to his base, he ordered his radio operator to bale out. Then he skilfully flew the smoking Beaufighter to the naval station at Portela. As soon as he had landed and shut down, he left the aircraft, thinking that the oil-starved engine might still burst into flames. As he got to the hatch, he tripped over his radio operator! The terrified crewman had been too frightened to jump and had huddled by the hatch until Beja found him. He scooped him up and sprinted away from the oil-covered, smouldering Beau.

Peter Weston, an RAF navigator, flew in some of the last Beaufighter combat missions. While ferrying new Bristol Brigand strike aircraft out to Malaya to deal with the Communist insurgency in 1950, he flew almost a dozen missions in the Beaufighter's rear cockpit, familiarizing himself with the terrain and operations. Once he saw how best to conduct operations against the rebels, he then trained the former Beau crews in the new Bristol aircraft. He recalls, 'The Beau would overheat in a hurry if you dawdled on the ground for any length of time. In the hot, humid climate of Malaya, we didn't mess about once we started engines.'

The last Beaufighters to fly were based at RAF Selatar, Singapore, in May 1960. Selatar had a reputation for seeing off many famous aircraft – the Spitfire, the Mosquito and the Short Sunderland flying boat all flew their last flight at this station. Two Beaus trundled about serving as target tugs until at last their time came. On 16 May 1960, a last hurrah of a formation flight around the area showed the Beau in its element for the final time. After landing, they were immediately scrapped. Thus, the Beaufighter served a full military career of twenty years, more than justifying the RAF's belief in the big fighter project.

Bristol Beaufighter Mk VIf Specifications

Wing Span	57ft 10in
Length	41ft 4in
Height	15ft 10in
Weight Empty	14,800lb
Maximum Weight	20,500lb
Speed	305mph at sea level; 320mph at 10,000ft
Service ceiling	19,000ft
Range	1,400 miles
Powerplants	Two Bristol Hercules VI sleeve-valve radials
Armament	Four 20mm Hispano cannons, six .303 calibre machine-guns.

417th member James K. Pence penned the feelings of the squadron about the Beau in his poem entitled:

It Ain't A RAFFING Matter
or
I told Orville. I told Wilbur. It'll never ...

The Bloody Beau's a work of art

Dashed off in haste and panic

By Britishers whose prior job

Was building the Titanic

The dynamics of this aero

Were patterned by the brick

If one Bristol ceased its churning

You could well be up a crick

The man up front aghast, amazed

At a total loss

The man behind bewildered

Staring at a Maltese Cross

Out of rig
Unbalanced
A survivor just the same
The bloody, lovely Beau
A beaut
A bitch
But what a dame!

APPENDIX III

The Northrop-61 Black Widow

A direct result of USAAF observers' experiences during the Battle of Britain and the subsequent Blitz, the Northrop P-61 Black Widow was the first purpose designed US night fighter. It was also the largest fighter ever used by the USAAF.

The Widow was a big but surprisingly agile fighter. Twin tail booms bordered the fuselage in a layout similar to Lockheed's P-38 Lightning. The 66ft wingspan incorporated very effective flap and spoiler systems for responsive manoeuvring. Powered by two Pratt & Whitney R-2800 eighteen cylinder engines, each putting out 2,100hp, the P-61 had a top speed of 425mph.

Equipped with the SCR-720 airborne intercept radar, the P-61 used both GCI control and freelance patrolling to find enemy aircraft. Once engaged, it had four forward-firing 20mm cannon and, in some models, up to four .50 calibre machine-guns in a revolving top turret. That turret resulted in severe stability problems in the early testing and production versions, so many of the P-61A models were manufactured without the turret. Later models sometimes had the turret, sometimes not. The 417th flew both variants, starting with A-models in March 1945.

The Widow had a pilot in the forward cockpit, a gunner (not often used,) in the top cockpit, and an R/O in the tail position. Planes without turrets had no need for a gunner, so some crews gave the gunner different tactical responsibilities.

James Van Voorhis recalls teaching his gunner to navigate during their flights over occupied Germany, thus relieving himself of the need both to fly and to keep detailed position reports of his travels. A second set of eyes on the chart and out of the window was a big help according to Van Voorhis.

Only four known Black Widows survive today. The National Museum of the US Air Force has a P-61C on display. The Mid-Atlantic Air Museum recovered a crashed P-61 from New Guinea in 1991 and is bringing the hulk back to display condition. The Smithsonian Air and Space Museum has one in their collection at the Udvar-Hazy facility. And strangely, a P-61C rests in the Chinese Aviation Museum in Beijing. It was salvaged (or taken, depending on the source,) at the end of World War II from a US squadron that was deactivated in China at the end of the war.

Northrop P-61A Black Widow Specifications:

Wing Span	66ft
Length	48ft 11in
Height	14ft 8in
Weight Empty	23,450lb
Maximum Weight	36,200lb
Speed	369 mph at 25,000ft
Service ceiling	43,250ft
Range	1,350 miles
Powerplants	Two Pratt & Whitney R-2800 eighteen-cylinder radials
Armament	Four 20mm cannons; some B/C models had turrets with up to four .50 calibre machine-guns.

APPENDIX IV

Record of 417th Squadron Aircraft

A/C No.	TYPE	COMMENTS
HV649	Beaufighter VI	On squadron records from 28/9/43 until 15/12/43.
41-12876	B-25C-NA	'Strawberry Roan', squadron hack aircraft.
KV823	Beaufighter VI	29/11/43 to 29/11/43. Squadron logged only two hours before it was destroyed.
KV910	Beaufighter VI	unknown.
KV911	Beaufighter VI	27/9/43 to 7/12/43.
KV913	Beaufighter VI	27/9/43 to 27/11/43. Exceeded fatigue life and returned to RAF.
KV923	Beaufighter VI	3/12/43 to 27/12/43.
KV928	Beaufighter VI	4/12/43 to 4/12/43.
KV932	Beaufighter VI	8/12/43 to 8/12/43. Bellylanded on delivery flight.
KV937	Beaufighter VI	28/12/43 to 1/1/44.
KV938	Beaufighter VI	29/11/43 to 18/3/44.
KV940	Beaufighter VI	11/12/43 to 20/1/44.
KV941	Beaufighter VI	13/11/43 to at least 13/4/44.
KV 961	Beaufighter VI	17/11/44 to at least 19/4/44.
KW151	Beaufighter VI	30/1/44 to at least 1/5/44.
KW158	Beaufighter VI	1/2/44 to 29/2/44.
443	B-25C	'Pizzonia', replacement hack for 'Strawberry Roan'.

KW161	Beaufighter VI	Unknown, listed on 19/4/44 combat report of Kirwan/Van Laecken.
KW191	Beaufighter VI	Turned in on 1/3/45 for P-61.
KW 197	Beaufighter VI	Unknown.
KW203	Beaufighter VI	Listed in maintenance reports, July 1944.
KZ488	Beaufighter VI	11/11/43 to 12/11/43.
LB595	Hurricane IIC	2/10/43 to 19/3/44.
BT287	Beaufighter VI	Unknown, listed as 2/11/44 mishap aircraft of Berryhill/Rogers, crew chief Anderton, all killed.
MM839	Beaufighter VI	Unknown, ditched by Lee/Potter, crew never found.
MM934	Beaufighter VI	Turned in 21/3/45 for P-61.
MM938	Beaufighter VI	Unknown, listed in squadron records on 31/10/44.
ND139	Beaufighter VI	Unknown, listed as 4/11/44 mishap aircraft of Howard/Mangone, crew survived.
ND164M	Beaufighter VI	25/11/43 to 23/3/44.
ND167	Beaufighter VI	1/1/44 to 9/3/44.
ND168	Beaufighter VI	29/11/43 to 11/3/44.
ND171	Beaufighter VI	7/12/43 to 16/12/43.
ND177	Beaufighter VI	25/11/43 to 6/2/44, mishap aircraft with Lee/Leonard, crew survived.
ND197	Beaufighter VI	Unknown, listed lost at sea on 15/11/44 with crew Devore/Grinnell after making contact with enemy.
ND203	Beaufighter VI	8/12/43 to 15/12/43.
ND204	Beaufighter VI	7/12/43 to 16/3/44, subsequently reacquired after mishap of Grange/Sunyar who ditched it on 25/9/44.
ND210	Beaufighter VI	9/12/43 to ?/5/44.

ND274	Beaufighter VI	Unknown, listed as mishap aircraft on 2/1/45, subsequently repaired.
ND278	Beaufighter VI	15/1/44 to 26/2/44.
ND280	Beaufighter VI	Unknown, listed as mishap aircraft on 28/11/44.
ND282	Beaufighter VI	16/2/44 to 18/3/44.
ND288	Beaufighter VI	Unknown, listed as mishap aircraft on 7/11/44, crew Grange/Sunyar baled out, survived.
ND296	Beaufighter VI	Unknown, listed as mishap aircraft on 5/12/44, pilot Davis badly burned but survived.
T3227	Beaufighter VI	Unknown, listed in records on 1/8/43.
V8450	Beaufighter VI	26/9/43 to 1/12/43.
V8558	Beaufighter VI	Unknown, listed as mishap aircraft 15/10/44, crew Howard/Mangone survived.
V8568	Beaufighter VI	Unknown, 28/12/44 aircraft of Campbell/McCullen for Ju 290 victory.
V8644	Beaufighter VI	Unknown, 4/2/45 listed as mishap aircraft of crew Howard/Mangone, crew unhurt.
V8716	Beaufighter VI	Unknown, listed as mishap aircraft on 18/1/45.
V8743M	Beaufighter VI	26/9/43 to 22/11/43.
V8745	Beaufighter VI	10/10/43 to 21/11/43.
V8760	Beaufighter VI	27/9/43 to 29/11/43.
V8806	Beaufighter VI	28/9/43 to 29/11/43.
V8812	Beaufighter VI	22/5/43, destroyed during 417th training in UK, crew McClain/Hendershott plus crew chief Dyer killed.
V8814M	Beaufighter VI	26/9/43 to 5/12/43.

V8819	Beaufighter VI	26/9/43 to 5/12/43.
V8821	Beaufighter VI	Unknown.
V8822	Beaufighter VI	11/10/43 to 5/12/43.
V8828	Beaufighter VI	Unknown, turned in for P-61, nicknamed 'Hi, Doc' with Bugs Bunny side art.
V8830	Beaufighter VI	Unknown.
V8831	Beaufighter VI	30/9/43 to 28/10/43.
V8834	Beaufighter VI	26/9/43 to 3/1/44.
42-39397	P-61A	Unknown, listed in squadron records on 4/7/45.
42-39420	P-61B	Unknown, 3/4/45 listed as mishap aircraft of Aubill/Hart, crew survived.
42-39420	P-61B	12/3/45 to unknown.
42-39487	P-61B	Unknown, listed in squadron records on 15/5/45.
42-39505	P-61B	22/3/45 to unknown.
42-39507	P-61B	Unknown.
42-39509	P-61B	22/4/45 to 9/6/45 when aircraft crashed, pilot Cooley killed.
42-39517	P-61B	14/4/45 to unknown.
42-39521	P-61B	Unknown, listed in squadron records on 18/5/45.
42-39533	P-61B	Unknown.
42-39533	P-61B	1/4/45 to unknown.
42-39535	P-61B	28/3/45 to at least 6/5/45.
42-39536	P-61B	18/3/45 to at least 20/4/45.
42-39559	P-61B	20/3/45 to unknown.
42-39563	P-61B	27/3/45 to at least 24/4/45.
42-39594	P-61B	Unknown, fitted with top turret, most 417th aircraft were not.
42-39606	P-61B	Unknown, fitted with top turret.
42-39628	P-61B	Unknown, fitted with top turret.
42-556?	P-61A	Unknown.

42-5568	P-61A	Unknown, listed in squadron records on 25/7/45.
42-5571	P-61A	Unknown, listed in squadron records on 3/7/45.
42-5585	P-61A	Unknown, listed in squadron records on 22/7/45.

Note: These are probably not all the aircraft that were ever on the 417th's wartime books, but records were sometimes not kept or retained during various moves and deactivations, or have been lost over the years.

APPENDIX V

417th Combat Victories and Narratives

Combat Victory Summary
Destroyed
4 Ju 88, 1 Ju 188, 1 Ju 290, 2 He 177
Probably destroyed
1 Do 217, 2 Ju 188, 1 Me 210/410
Damaged
7 Ju 88, 2 Ju 188, 2 unidentified.

NARRATIVE OF COMBAT, MORNING OF 28 MARCH 1944

OUR AIRCRAFT WAS AIRBORNE FROM LA SENIA, AFRICA AT 0505 HRS ON TENTACLE SWEEP MISSION, FREELANCE.

AT 0755 HRS OUR A/C SIGHTED A JU-88 FLYING AT DECK LEVEL ON HEADING OF 030 DEG DOING 280MPH.

OUR A/C IMMEDIATELY CORRECTED OVERTAKING SPEED AND REDUCED ALTITUDE FOR ATTACK POSITION. CHASE PROCEEDED AT DECK LEVEL WHEREUPON FROM 800YD. RANGE OUR A/C FIRED A SHORT BURST TO CHECK PATTERN AND AGAIN GIVING BURST CEASING FIRE AT 200FT. RANGE AND BREAKING AWAY EVADING ENEMY'S RETURN FIRE BUT OUR A/C SUSTAINED DAMAGE TO EXHAUST COLLECTION RING, PORT ENGINE AND PORT WING MAIN SPAN.

OUR AIRCRAFT'S ATTACK SUCCEEDED IN DAMAGING ENEMY AIRCRAFT REDUCING ITS PERFORMANCE AND WHICH WAS LATER DESTROYED BY ANOTHER FRIENDLY A/C.

CLAIM WAS MADE FOR AND VERIFIED AS ONE JU-88 DAMAGED BY F/O JEFFREY AND F/O HENDERSON-RO.

NARRATIVE OF COMBAT, MORNING OF 28 MARCH 1944

OUR AIRCRAFT WAS AIRBORNE FROM LA SENIA, AFRICA AT 0510 HRS. TO PERFORM A TENTACLE SWEEP MISSION, FREELANCE.

AT 0758 HRS. OUR A/C SIGHTED ONE JU-88 AT DECK LEVEL DOING 280MPH.

AT 0830 HRS ON HEADING OF 030 DEG. OUR A/C OPENED FIRE FROM 800 YDS AT DECK LEVEL OBSERVING PATTERN OF GUNFIRE AROUND THE ENEMY A/C. OUR A/C RECEIVED RETURN FIRE FROM ENEMY'S DORSAL GUNS SUSTAINING NO DAMAGE. ENEMY AIRCRAFT THEN HEADED TOWARD COAST OF FRANCE.

NO CLAIM WAS MADE.

NARRATIVE OF COMBAT, NIGHT OF 31 MARCH, 1944

OUR AIRCRAFT WAS SCRAMBLED AND AIRBORNE AT 2245 AND CONTROLLED BY 'PERFORM' CONTROL STATION.

'PERFORM' VECTORED OUR A/C WITHIN 2 MILES OF ENEMY A/C. SIGHTED ENEMY A/C AT 2350 HRS. AND IDENTIFIED IT AS A JU-88 APPROXIMATELY 55 MILES NORTH NORTHWEST OF CAPE TENES, AFRICA ON HEADING OF 240YDS AT HEIGHT OF 50FT.

RECEIVED NO RETURN FIRE FROM ENEMY A/C WHO WAS CONTINUOUSLY TAKING VERY HARD EVASIVE ACTION AT DECK LEVEL.

OUR A/C CEASED FIRING AT 130YDS ON FIRST BURST DUE TO EVASIVE TACTICS BREAKING LINE OF SIGHT, THEREFORE OUR A/C KEPT ON. GOT ENEMY IN SIGHTS AGAIN AND MADE SECOND BURST FROM 110-115 YDS BREAKING OFF AT 75YDS OR SLIGHTLY LESS.

CLAIM WAS MADE FOR AND VERIFIED AS ONE JU-88 DAMAGED BY F/O JEFFREY AND F/O HENDERSON-RO. (CLAIM LATER UPGRADED TO DESTROYED)

NARRATIVE OF COMBAT, NIGHT OF 1 MAY 1944

OUR A/C WAS ON NORTH PATROL ALMOST AT THE EXTREME END OF THAT LEG OF THE PATROL WHEN IT WAS RECALLED AND TURNED OVER TO 'BANDBOX' GCI/COL STATION AT 2130 HRS.

WHILE BEING VECTORED SOUTH, OUR A/C, WHILE STILL 15 MILES N/W OF ELBA, OBTAINED A VISUAL OF A HOSTILE A/C AND IDENTIFIED IT AS A JU-88. THE HOSTILE WAS TRAVELLING SOUTH AT ANGELS 13. OUR A/C AT THE TIME WAS HEADED APPROX. SOUTHWEST.

OUR A/C THEN SWUNG AROUND TO PORT AND OBTAINEDA.I.CONTACT. HOSTILE HAD APPARENTLY STARTED MODERATE EVASIVE ACTION ON FIRST VISUAL.

OUR A/C CLOSED TO 600FT. GAVE A SHORT BURST OF APPROX. TWO SECONDS DURATION WITH FIVE DEG. DEFLECTION AND OBSERVED STRIKE ON THE E/A'S PORT ENGINE, PORT WING AND THENCE TO FUSELAGE.

OUR A/C CONTINUED TURNING AND GAVE ANOTHER BURST OF APPROX. FROM TWO TO TWO AND ONE HALF SECONDS DURATION, WITH AN ESTIMATED TWENTY DEG. DEFLECTION AND OBSERVED NO STRIKES.

RECEIVED RETURN FIRE BUT NO DAMAGE WAS SUSTAINED BY OWN A/C. AFTER LOSING A.I. CONTACT, CONTROLLER WAS UNABLE TO GIVE FURTHER HELP AS ENEMY A/C WAS BEHIND PIANOSA AND PLOT FADED AND WAS NOT PICKED UP UNTIL HOSTILE WAS WELL ON WAY HOME. HOSTILE WAS W/T'ING THAT HE WAS RETURNING ON ONE ENGINE AND IN TROUBLE.

E/A WAS TRAVELLING AT APPROX. 230MPH WHEN FIRST SIGHTED. OWN A/C WHEN CLOSING IN, CAME FROM ANGELS 10 TO SAME LEVEL AS E/A, 130FT.

CLAIM WAS MADE FOR AND VERIFIED AS ONE JU-88 DAMAGED BY LT JACK KIRWAN AND F/O JOE VAN LAECKEN-RO.

NARRATIVE OF COMBAT, NIGHT OF 3 MAY 1944

ON THE NIGHT OF 3 MAY, 1944, 'RAGTOY' CONTROL

STATION WAS CONTROLLING OUR A/C WHICH WAS PATROLLING BETWEEN PIANOSA AND CAPRAIA, WEST OF ELBA, AT 1000.

AT ABOUT 2210 HRS 'RAGTOY' VECTORED OUR A/C ONTO A HOSTILE.

OUR A/C MADE A.I. CONTACT AT 3 ½ MILE RANGE AND OBTAINING A VISUAL, IDENTIFIED THE HOSTILE AS A JU-88.

OUR A/C CLOSED IN TO 600 ON THE SAME LEVEL AS THE E/A AND GAVE A ONE SECOND BURST FROM 10 DEG STBD. THE TARGET BROKE HARD TO PORT AND CONTACT WAS LOST. ANOTHER VECTOR WAS GIVEN AND MAKING A QUICK CLOSE-IN TO 700FT, OUR A/C FIRED TWO TWO SECOND BURSTS. THE JU-88 AGAIN BROKE HARD TO PORT AND DOWN, SWINGING BACK THROUGH STBD AND FROM R0 DEG. DEFLECTION, OUR A/C FIRED ANOTHER SHORT BURST. THE E/A AT THIS TIME WAS APPROX. 400/500FT HIGH.

VISUAL CONTACT WAS LOST SO OUR A/C CLOSED IN ON ANOTHER INTERCEPTION AND OBTAINING VISUAL CONTACT, GAVE ANOTHER THREE SECOND BURST THEN LOST THE TARGET OVER PIANOSA. NO STRIKES WERE OBSERVED ON THE ENEMY A/C ALTHOUGH THE PATTERN WAS WELL CENTERED AROUND THE A/C.

THE ENEMY WAS TAKING VIOLENT EVASIVE ACTION AND KEPT ORBITING CONTINUOUSLY. OUR A/C RECEIVED RETURN FIRE CONTINUOUSLY AND SUSTAINED MINOR DAMAGE CONSISTING OF ONE 9MM HOLE IN THE STBD EXHAUST RING. THE RETURN TO BASE WAS MADE WITHOUT INCIDENT OTHER THAN A ROUGH STBD ENGINE.

NO CLAIM WAS MADE.

NARRATIVE OF COMBAT, MORNING OF 9 MAY 1944

AT 0240 HRS OUR A/C WAS SCRAMBLED TO INTERCEPT A HOSTILE A/C PLOTTED APPROACHING CORSICA FROM THE SOUTH.

IMMEDIATELY UPON BEING AIRBORNE, 'RAGTOY' CONTROL STATION TOOK OVER GIVING OUR A/C A

VECTOR CALCULATED TO INTERCEPT THE ENEMY A/C. 'RAGTOY' REPORTED THE BANDIT AT ELEVEN O'CLOCK. RANGE, FIVE MILES.

APPROX. ONE MINUTE LATER, OUR A/C OBTAINED A.I. CONTACT AND REDUCED ITS LEVEL TO 100', THE BANDIT BEING AT THAT LEVEL, AND CLOSED IN OH THE TARGET AT 250-260MPH.

NO EVASIVE ACTION WAS TAKEN BY THE ENEMY A/C OTHER THAN GENTLE TURNS. THE CHASE WAS IN GENERAL IN AN EASTERLY DIRECTION. AT APPROX. 0251, CONTROL REPORTED THAT THEY COULD GIVE NO HELP AT THE MOMENT. OUR A/C'S CAPTAIN GAVE 'CONTACT' IN SPITE OF POSSIBLE GERMAN MONITOR-ING OF THE R/T.

THREE TIMES WITHIN THE NEXT TWO MINUTES, 'RAGTOY' WARNED OUR A/C THAT IT WAS APPROACH-ING BACKWASH AND TO TURN BACK RATHER THAN TO CROSS, HOWEVER, IN SPITE OF THIS, OUR A/C MAIN-TAINED VISUAL CONTACT. VISUAL CONTACT AT THIS TIME CONSISTED OF FLEETING VISUALS ON THE BANDIT AT A RANGE OF 2000', WHICH BECAME CONSTANT AFTER CLOSING IN TO 1500'.

AT THIS TIME, LAND BECAME VISIBLE AND DEAD AHEAD, [LATER IDENTIFIED AS THE HILL ON THE SOUTHEAST TIP OF ELBA WHICH WAS ENEMY HELD TERRITORY]. AS THE BANDIT WAS FLYING ALMOST DIRECTLY AWAY FROM THE MOON, WHICH WAS FULL, OUR A/C ATTACKED FROM THE SAME LEVEL AS TARGET'S, IN ORDER TO STAY OUT OF THE MOON-PATH ON THE WATER AND YET AVOID BEING SILHOUETTED AGAINST THE MOON.

AT 600FT RANGE IDENTIFIED THE BANDIT AS A JU-88 AND OPENED FIRE FROM DEAD ASTERN. NO RESULTS WERE OBSERVED FROM OUR A/C'S FIRST BURST OF APPROXIMATELY ONE SECOND DURATION. THE BANDIT OPENED FIRE FROM ITS TURRET ALMOST SIMULTANEOUSLY, ALL OF ITS TRACERS PASSING TO STBD.

CLOSING IN ON E/A, OUR A/C FIRED A THREE SECOND

BURST AND OBSERVED HIGH EXPLOSIVE BURSTS ON THE STBD WING IN LINE WITH THE ENGINE NACELLE AND BROKE OFF ITS ATTACK AT A RANGE OF 50YDS. AS OUR A/C BROKE OFF, HOSTILE'S UPPER TURRET GUNNER FIRED ANOTHER BURST AT OUR A/C WHICH WAS INACCURATE.

ON TURNING BACK TOWARD THE HOSTILE, VISUAL WAS LOST. APPARENTLY THE E/A WAS BETWEEN OUR A/C AND LAND OUR A/C WAS UNABLE TO REGAIN A.I. CONTACT DUE TO HEAVY GROUND RETURNS AND CHASE WAS THEREFORE ABANDONED, ABOUT 2½ MILES FROM THE COAST OF ITALY.

CLAIM WAS MADE FOR AND VERIFIED FOR ONE JU-88 DAMAGED BY CAPT C.R. MCCRAY AND F/O R. D. HAMILTON-RO.

NARRATIVE OF COMBAT, NIGHT OF 9 MAY 1944

OUR A/C WAS ON PATROL OFF CAP CURSE, PIANOSA AND CAPRAIA BEING CONTROLLED BY 'BLACKTOP' (SECTOR).

AT 2150 HRS, OUR A/C WAS TAKEN OVER BY 'BANDBOX' CONTROL STATION AND VECTORED AFTER BOGEY HEADING SOUTH AT 12 MILES. BOGEY THEN TURNED NORTH AND OUR A/C OBTAINED AI CONTACT AT 2315 HRS AT 2½ MILES. OUR A/C'S ANGELS AT THE TIME WAS 100FT AND BOGEY WAS AT 40 FT TRAVELLING ABOUT 210 MPH.

AT 230MPH OUR A/C CLOSED IN TO 1500' WITH TARGET STILL READING ABOVE AND CLOSED TO PAST MINIMUM RANGE CLIMBING TO 300FT.

TARGET THEN OPENED FIRE FROM DIRECTLY BELOW (APPARENTLY AT PRECISELY THE SAME TIME WE CLIMBED, THE E/A THROTTLED BACK AND WENT DOWN TO GET US TO OVERSHOOT) AND OUR A/C BROKE TO PORT AND ORBITED.

TARGET THEN DISAPPEARED AND OUR A/C COULDN'T PICK UP A.I. CONTACT. OUR A/C RECEIVED ANOTHER VECTOR ONTO BANDIT BUT STILL COULDN'T OBTAIN VISUAL ALTHOUGH A.I. CONTACT WAS AGAIN

OBTAINED AT 2½ MILES. THIS WAS LOST WHEN TARGET DODGED AROUND THE SOUTHWEST CORNER OF ELBA AT 100FT. ALTITUDE, TRAVELLING AT APPROX. 230MPH AND OUR A/C AT 230-240MPH.

NO 'WINDOW' WAS ENCOUNTERED AND A.I. AND VECTORING BY CONTROL STATION WAS GOOD.

THERE WAS NO CLAIM MADE. CONTROLLER ADVISED THIS AIRCREW ON LANDING THAT THE ENEMY A/C WAS RECEIVING CONSTANT HELP, HAVING REPORTED BEING IN TROUBLE AND HAVING DIFFICULTY DUE TO BEING CHASED.

NARRATIVE OF COMBAT, MORNING OF 13 MAY 1944

WHILE ON SOUTHERN PATROL, MORNING OF 13 MAY 1944, 'TOOTPASTE' CONTROL STATION ADVISED OUR A/C THAT PLOT WAS BELIEVED FRIENDLY, SO OUR A/C INVESTIGATED WITH CAUTION.

OBTAINED A.I. CONTACT AT 0200 HRS AND FOLLOWED IT IN FROM 4 MILES RANGE. VISUAL WAS OBTAINED AT 1500' AND AT A RANGE OF 1000', TENTA-TIVELY IDENTIFIED BOGEY AS A WELLINGTON BOMBER, INFLUENCED BY CONTROLLER'S STATEMENT THAT IT WAS BELIEVED FRIENDLY.

OUR A/C SPENT FOUR MINUTES IN A VERY VULNERA-BLE POSITION DURING WHICH TIME THE BOGEY SHOWED NO IFF. AT ABOUT 500' RANGE, OUR A/C IDEN-TIFIED BOGEY AS AN HE-177. OUR A/C THEN PULLED UP, (SPEED APPROX. 220, E/A'S 210-220) AND OPENED FIRE, RECEIVING APPROX. FOUR BURSTS OF RETURN FIRE FROM THE TAIL POSITION, INFLICTING DAMAGE IN OUR A/C'S STBD WING. STBD AND PORT STABILIZERS.

OUR A/C FIRED TWO MORE BURSTS OF TWO TO THREE SECONDS EACH. THEN THE ENEMY A/C IN THREE SUC-CESSIVE PEEL-OFFS REDUCED

ALTITUDE FROM 8000' TO 300'.

AFTER E/A'S FIRST PEEL-OFF, OUR A/C GOT IN A TWO TO THREE SECOND BURST AND OBSERVED HITS ON E/A'S VERTICAL FIN. AT THE BOTTOM OF E/A'S PEEL-OFF, HE PULLED UP SHARPLY, THEN WENT INTO A DIVING

TURN, ESCAPING OUR A.I. COVERAGE. A.I. CONTACT WAS NOT REGAINED.

'TOOTHPASTE' THEN PUT OUR A/C BACK UP TO ANGELS 7 AND AT ABOUT 0235, VECTORED IT ONTO A BOGEY. AT ABOUT 0245, OBTAINED A.I. CONTACT AND CLOSED IN TO ABOUT 1500' AND OBTAINED A VISUAL. SPEED OF OUR A/C WAS 210-220 MPH AND E/A'S 210-220. SUN-SIGHT WAS U/S AND SPARE BULBS PUT IN BURNED OUT AS FAST AS REPLACED, SO OUR A/C FIRED BY APPROXIMATION.

THE ENEMY A/C WAS FLYING DIRECTLY INTO THE MOON AND WAS VERY HARD TO SPOT AND AT ABOUT 1200' TO 1500' RANGE, DROPPED A SMALL QUANTITY OF 'WINDOW'. OUR A/ C THEN IDENTIFIED E/A AS AN HE-177 AND CLOSED IN TO ABOUT 200 YARDS. THE FIRST TWO SECOND BURST GAVE NO VISIBLE RESULTS AND E/A COMMENCED EVASIVE ACTION, CONSISTING OF MEDIUM AND HARD TURNS WITH NO APPRECIABLE CHANGE IN ALTITUDE ON THE SECOND BURST OF APPROX. THREE SECONDS DURATION, DURING WHICH THE CANNON QUIT FIRING, A NUMBER OF 20MM STRIKES WERE OBSERVED ON THE INNER SIDE OF THE E/A'S STBD NACELLE. FLAMES SHOWED WHICH PERSISTED FOR ABOUT FIVE SECONDS BUT THEN DIED OUT.

OUR A/C'S WINDSCREEN WAS COVERED WITH AN OILY MIXTURE. AFTER THE CANNON QUIT FIRING, CONTINUED FIRING ON .303'S. IN SEVERAL 2 TO 3 SECOND BURSTS, BALANCE OF OWN A/C'S AMMUNITION WAS EXPENDED, AT WHICH TIME E/A'S SPEED DROPPED TO 135 MPH AND EVASIVE ACTION CEASED, APPARENTLY DUE TO LOSS OF STBD ENGINES.

ACTION TERMINATED APPROX. 35-40 MILES SOUTHEAST OF BORGO A/D [CORSICA] AND E/A WAS LOSING ALTITUDE AT SUCH A RATE THAT HE COULD NOT REACH TERRITORY FRIENDLY TO HIM, LET ALONE MAKE A LANDING. THERE WAS NO RETURN FIRE FROM THE SECOND E/A AT ANY TIME.

CLAIM WAS MADE FOR AND VERIFIED AS ONE HE-177

PROBABLE AND ONE HE-177 DAMAGED BY CAPT C.R. MCCRAY AND F/O R.D. HAMILTON-RO.

NARRATIVE OF COMBAT, NIGHT OF 13 MAY 1944

OUR A/C TOOK OFF AT 2210 ON NORTH PATROL, CON-TROLLED BY 'BLACKTOP'.

AT 2220, 'BANDBOX' TOOK OVER CONTROL AND AT 2240 A BANDIT WAS REPORTED 30 MILES NORTH ON A SOUTHERLY VECTOR.

'BANDBOX' TURNED OUR A/C ON A NORTHWEST VECTOR AND FINALLY BROUGHT OUR A/C INTO SUCH A POSITION AS TO ENABLE IT TO OBTAIN A.I. CONTACT. THIS WAS AT 2255.

OUR A/C THEN CLOSED IN FROM 3 MILES AT 240-260 MPH AND IDENTIFIED BANDIT AS A JU-88 AT 300FT ALTITUDE RANGE 600FT. AHEAD.

OUR A/C THEN SLOWED TO E/A'S SPEED APPROX. 220MPH AND AT 600-700FT. RANGE. GAVE TWO 2 SECOND BURSTS FROM DEAD ASTERN OBSERVING A FLASH ON E/A'S STARBOARD WING. E/A GAVE RETURN FIRE AND TURNED OFF TO PORT. A.I. CONTACT WAS THEN LOST.

OUR A/C THEN ORBITED, CALLING FOR A VECTOR BUT 'BANDBOX' COULD NOT HELP, OUR A/C FINALLY PICKING UP E/A AGAIN WHICH WAS AT 4 MILES. OWN A/C THEN CHASED E/A FOR APPROX. TEN MINUTES, CLOSING TO APPROX. 2000FT. WITH E/A READING BELOW. OUR A/C'S ALTITUDE AT THIS TIME WAS FROM TWO TO THREE HUNDRED FEET. E/A'S SPEED WAS APPROXIMATELY 220MPH AND E/A WAS UTILIZING HARD ORBITS FOR EVASIVE ACTION. OUR A/ C'S SPEED AT THIS TIME WAS FROM 240 TO 260MPH AND WHEN CLOSING IN, HAD TO DROP WHEELS TO AVOID OVER-SHOOTING THE E/A.

OUR A/C'S PORT WHEEL DROPPED JUST OUT OF THE NACELLE AND NO FURTHER, HYDRAULIC SYSTEM BEING U/S. OUR A/C CONTINUED CHASE IN SPITE OF THE PORT WHEEL HANGING HALF-WAY OUT OF THE NACELLE BUT LOST THE ENEMY A/C BELOW AND OFF

TO STARBOARD.

OUR A/C WAS UNABLE TO REGAIN A.I. CONTACT OR VISUAL. UPON CALLING 'BLACKTOP', IT WAS CALLED TO BASE.

NO DAMAGE WAS SUSTAINED BY OUR A/C THROUGH THE RETURN FIRE OF THE E/A'S DORSAL TURRET, HOWEVER, FAILURE OF THE HYDRAULIC SYSTEM NECESSITATED A CRASH-LANDING UPON ARRIVAL TO BASE. THERE WERE NO INJURIES TO PERSONNEL.

CLAIM WAS MADE FOR AND VERIFIED AS ONE JU-88 DAMAGED BY CAPT J.S.M. LEE AND F/O L.R. POTTER-RO.

NARRATIVE OF COMBAT, NIGHT OF 30 JUNE 1944

OUR A/C WAS AIRBORNE AT 2120 FOR FREELANCE PATROL WITH 'BANDBOX'.

AFTER PATROLLING AT WILL FOR SOMETIME, CONTROL CALLED AND STATED THAT A BANDIT WAS PLOTTED 50 MILES NORTH, HEADING SOUTH ALONG THE ITALIAN COAST. 'BANDBOX' GAVE A CUT-OFF VECTOR, AT WHICH TIME OUR A/C WAS FLYING AT 500FT. THE FIRST RANGE GIVEN WAS FIVE MILES, HOWEVER, A.I. CONTACT COULD NOT BE OBTAINED SO OUR A/C WENT DOWN TO 200FT.

AT 2323, FIRST A.I. CONTACT WAS OBTAINED AT A RANGE OF 2 ½ MILES WITH BANDIT READING BELOW. OUR A/C FOLLOWED BANDIT ON A SOUTHERLY COURSE, VARYING SOUTHEAST TO SOUTHWEST. THE MOON WAS BRIGHT AND AT A RANGE OF ONE MILE, ALTITUDE OF 100FT. OWN A/C HIT THE BANDIT'S PROP-WASH. EVEN THOUGH THE BANDIT WAS IN THE MOON-PATH OUR A/C COULD NOT OBTAIN A VISUAL.

AT A RANGE OF 1500FT. ALTITUDE 50-75FT., VISUAL CONTACT WAS OBTAINED AND THE BANDIT WAS IMME-DIATELY RECOGNIZED AS A JU-88 BY THE BULBOUS NOSE AND LONG FUSELAGE AFT OF THE WINGS. FLYING AT AN ALTITUDE OF FROM 75 TO 100FT., AND IN THE BANDIT'S PROPWASH, OUR A/C CLOSED IN TO A VERY CLOSE RANGE IN ORDER TO MAKE CERTAIN THAT HIS BULLETS FOUND THEIR INTENDED MARK.

HOWEVER, AS OUR A/C WAS CLOSING IN, BANDIT TURNED EAST INTO THE DARK PART OF THE SKY AND AS HE WAS TURNING, OUR A/C OPENED FIRE WITH A QUITE LONG (3 TO 4 SECOND) BURST WITH 1½ RING DEFLECTION. NO STRIKES WERE OBSERVED AND VISUAL CONTACT WAS LOST AS SOON AS THE BANDIT LEFT THE MOON-PATH.

UPON BANDIT'S TURNING INTO THE DARK, OUR A/C WAS LEFT IN THE MOON-PATH AND RECEIVED RETURN FIRE FROM E/A. ALL THAT OUR A/C'S CREW COULD SEE WAS THE RED TRACER FROM THE BANDIT'S TWIN MACHINE GUNS. POSITION OF THE GUN EMPLACE-MENTS COULD NOT BE DETERMINED DUE TO DARKNESS, HOWEVER, NO HITS WERE SUSTAINED ON OUR A/C.

BANDIT WAS FOLLOWED ON A NORTH/NORTHEAST COURSE FOR APPROX. TEN MINUTES AT AN ALTITUDE ON A.I. CONTACT. RANGE 2 MILES TO 1,600FT, WITHOUT ANOTHER VISUAL BEING OBTAINED. NEAR THE END OF THE CHASE, BANDIT STARTED TO CLIMB, CLIMBING TO ABOUT 500FT. ACCORDING TO THE RADIO OBSERVER IN OUR A/C.

OUR A/C STAYED AT 100FT. PLANNING ON COMING UNDERNEATH THE BANDIT AND GETTING A CLOSE-IN BURST. AS SOON AS THE BANDIT REACHED 500FT. HE PEELED-OFF AND DISAPPEARED OFF OUR A/C'S SCOPE INTO THE GROUND SCATTER OFF THE COAST OF ITALY. OUR A/C LOST THE BANDIT, AS DID ALL GROUND STATIONS, APPROX. 15 MILES DUE SOUTH OF PIANOSA.

NO CLAIM WAS MADE IN-AS-MUCH AS THERE WERE NO STRIKES OBSERVED.

NARRATIVE OF COMBAT, MORNING OF 4 JULY 1944

OUR A/C WAS SCRAMBLED AT 0210, 20 MINUTES AHEAD OF PATROL PREVIOUSLY SCHEDULED, TO CHASE A BANDIT.

'BANDBOX' TOOK OVER CONTROL AND VECTORED OUR A/C UNTIL A.I. CONTACT WAS MADE ON BANDIT ABOUT 3 MILES SOUTHEAST OF GORGONA ISLAND.

VISUAL WAS OBTAINED ALMOST IMMEDIATELY ON THE BANDIT, SLIGHTLY ABOVE AND ON OUR A/C'S PORT, AT AN ALTITUDE OF 150FT., RANGE 1,000 FT. BANDIT'S ALTITUDE, WHEN SIGHTED, WAS 200FT. WITH AN AIRSPEED OF 210MPH.

BANDIT TURNED TO PORT AND FIRED A SHORT BURST FROM HIS DORSAL POSITION. OUR A/C LOST VISUAL CONTACT AGAINST THE DARK MASS OF GORGONA ISLAND BUT FOLLOWED THE E/A WITH A.I. CONTACT AROUND TO THE WEST SIDE OF THE ISLAND, ABOUT ½ MILE OFFSHORE. VISUAL WAS AGAIN OBTAINED ON THE BANDIT BELOW AND TO PORT, RANGE 1200FT.

THE BANDIT FIRED TWO SHORT BURSTS AND TURNED ONTO A VECTOR OF 030 DEG. WHICH PUT HIS TAIL DIRECTLY TOWARDS THE MOON. OUR A/C MOVED TO STARBOARD TO GET OUT OF THE MOON-PATH AND CLOSE IN FOR A DEFLECTION SHOT.

THE BANDIT FIRED ANOTHER SHORT BURST OF ½ SECOND DURATION. VISUAL WAS THEN LOST IN A CLOUD SHADOW AND A.I. CONTACT WHICH HAD BEEN LOST IN MOVING STARBOARD COULD NOT BE REGAINED.

OUR A/C THEN SEARCHED THE AREA WITH A.I. FOR ANOTHER FIVE MINUTES BUT WITHOUT SUCCESS. THE BANDIT HAD FADED FROM THE GROUND CONTROL STATION SO OWN A/C HEADED BACK TO PREVIOUSLY ASSIGNED PATROL. NONE OF THE BANDIT'S FIRE, ALL OF WHICH WAS FROM TWIN DORSAL GUNS, WAS EFFECTIVE. BANDIT WAS IDENTIFIED AS A JU-88.

NO CLAIM WAS MADE.

NARRATIVE OF COMBAT, MORNING OF 6 JULY 1944

OUR A/C AIRBORNE AT 0040 FOR PATROL WITH 'STRAIGHTLACE' CONTROL STATION.

AT ABOUT 0140, 'STRAIGHTLACE' ASKED FOR A/C TO INVESTIGATE A PLOT REPORTED FRIENDLY BUT SUSPECTED OF OTHER IDENTITY BY CONTROLLER. OUR A/C WAS VECTORED IN ON AN EASTERLY DIRECTION AND CONTROLLER THOUGHT THAT HE HAD LOST R/T

CONTACT WHEN OUR A/C'S STARBOARD TRANSMITTER BECAME U/S. SWITCHED TO CHANNEL 'B' AND RESUMED INTERCEPTION.

THREE STARBOARD TURNS PUT OUR A/C ONTO 'FRIENDS' COURSE WHICH WAS THEN 240 DEG. PLOT WAS CHANGED TO BOGEY AND EVERY EFFORT WAS MADE TO OVERTAKE HIM. OUR A/C THEN MADE ALTITUDE OF 200FT., SPEED 295MPH. WHEN RANGE WAS DECREASED TO 4 MILES, OUR A/C THROTTLED BACK SLIGHTLY.

AT THREE MILES, OUR A/C AGAIN THROTTLED BACK, REDUCING SPEED TO 260 WHEN CONTROL REPORTED BOGEY W/4 MILES DEAD AHEAD. OUR A/C THEN THROTTLED BACK AS FAR AS POSSIBLE WITHOUT CAUSING EXHAUST FLASH.

WITH AIRSPEED REDUCED TO 220, OUR A/C OBTAINED A VISUAL BUT NO A.I. CONTACT ON A JU-88 FLYING A PARALLEL COURSE ABOUT 1000 FT. TO PORT ABOUT 50FT. ABOVE, RANGE ABOUT 1200FT.

VISUALS WERE ALMOST SIMULTANEOUS AND BOTH A/C TURNED TOWARDS EACH OTHER. BANDIT FIRED A ½ SECOND BURST FROM HIS DORSAL TURRET WHILE IN A BANK HEADED TOWARD OUR A/C. THE BANDIT PASSED DIRECTLY OVER OUR A/C, ABOUT 50FT. ABOVE AND OUR A/C ROLLED INTO A HARD STARBOARD TURN, BANDIT INTO HARD PORT, BOTH CLIMBING SLIGHTLY.

NEITHER OF THE A/C COULD TURN INSIDE THE OTHER TO OBTAIN A BURST WHILE FLYING NEARLY HEAD-ON. OUR A/C PASSED OVER THE BANDIT, ABOUT 30FT. (CLOSE ENOUGH TO DETERMINE THE UPPER SURFACE OF BANDIT WAS PAINTED A LIGHT COLOR WITH DARKER CAMOUFLAGE). BANDIT'S DORSAL GUNS FIRED ANOTHER VERY SHORT BURST JUST AFTER HE PASSED BENEATH.

OUR A/C CONTINUED TO TURN TO REMAIN IN THE DARK SIDE OF THE SKY AND, POSSIBLE, COME IN ON THE BANDIT'S TAIL. VISUAL WAS LOST IN THE TURN AND A.I. HAD SHOWN NO INDICATION OF BANDIT (OUR

RADAR TECHNICIANS BELIEVE THIS WAS DUE TO TEM-PERATURE INVERSION), AND CONTROL COULD GIVE NO HELP.

OUR A/C HEADED BACK TOWARDS THE PATROL AREA. BANDIT WAS AGAIN PLOTTED AND OUR A/C CHASED HIM, AT RANGES VARYING FROM 60 MILES TO 2 MILES, SOUTH 30 MILES OFF WEST COAST OF CORSICA, THRU A WIDE SWEEP TO THE WEST AND BACK NORTH. EXACT POSITIONS WERE NOT KNOWN. AT APPROX. 0315 ANOTHER OF OUR A/C TOOK UP THE CHASE, HOWEVER, SECOND A/C MADE NO CONTACTS, EITHER VISUAL OR WITH AI.

NO CLAIM WAS MADE.

NARRATIVE OF COMBAT. MORNING OF 7 JULY, 1944.

OUR A/C WAS AIRBORNE AT 0140 FOR PATROL WITH 'SPOTLIGHT' CONTROL STATION.

AT APPROX. 0210, WAS VECTORED TO A DESIGNATED POINT AND TOLD TO CONTACT 'STRAIGHTLACE' CONTROL WHICH WAS DONE WITH DIFFICULTY.

A/C WAS THEN VECTORED ONTO A BANDIT AT 0245. CONTACT WAS MADE AT 0320, 400FT. ALTITUDE, RANGE FOUR MILES SLIGHTLY TO PORT.

OUR A/C TURNED IN TOWARDS TARGET AND CONTACT FADED IN SEA AND ATMOSPHERIC RETURNS WHICH WERE VERY HEAVY. OUR A/C OBTAINED A VISUAL ON THE BANDIT, WHO WAS FLYING IN A SOUTHWEST DIRECTION. THE BANDIT WAS COMING INTO THE MOON-PATH AHEAD AND BELOW AT AN ALTITUDE OF FROM 50 TO 100FT. OUR A/C WAS AT 300FT., SPEED 230MPH, WITH BANDIT'S SPEED PLACED AT 220MPH.

VISUAL WAS OBTAINED AT 032 AND OUR A/C DOVE SLIGHTLY, TURNING TO STARBOARD AND GAVE A THREE TO FOUR SECOND BURST WITH ABOUT 30 DEG. DEFLECTION. HIGH EXPLOSIVE STRIKES WERE OBSERVED ON THE ENEMY A/C'S STARBOARD WING ROOT AND FUSELAGE. THE E/A GAVE INTENSE RETURN FIRE AND OUR A/C BROKE TO PORT LOSING VISUAL

CONTACT.

'STRAIGHTLACE' CONTROL COULD GIVE OUR A/C NO FURTHER HELP SINCE THE PLOT HAD FADED FROM THEIR SCOPE AT THAT TIME AND DID NOT REAPPEAR.

CLAIM WAS MADE FOR AND VERIFIED AS ONE JU-88 DAMAGED BY LT HILL AND F/O HEINECKE-RO.

NARRATIVE OF COMBAT. MORNING OF 8 JULY, 1944.

AIRBORNE AT MIDNIGHT, OUR A/C FREE-LANCED, STANDING BY ON 'BANDBOX' CONTROL STATION.

AT 0055, CONTROL STATED THAT A PLOT OF A BANDIT WAS POSSIBLE, HOWEVER. OUR A/C WAS UNABLE TO ACKNOWLEDGE SO A/C WENT OVER TO 'BLACKTOP' (SECTOR CONTROL) AND WAS VECTORED ABOUT UNTIL RELIEVED BY ANOTHER OF OUR A/C. (THIS A/C OBTAINED NO CONTACT ON BANDIT).

AT 0145, OUR A/C WAS AGAIN AIR-BORNE AND FLEW A CONTINUAL VECTOR UNTIL BOGEY WAS REPORTED TO THE SOUTH-EAST.

AT 0210, 'SETSQUARE' CONTROL STATION VECTORED OUR A/C INTO A.I. RANGE AND CHASE WAS COMMENCED AT 500FT. ALTITUDE WITH TARGET AT THREE MILES, 350 DEG. ABOVE. BOTH A/C MOVED INTO 'BANDBOX' CONTROL AREA AND CHASE CONTINUED WITH A.I. EQUIPMENT.

OUR A/C, IN CLIMBING TO 7500FT. (TARGET LEVEL), LOST TARGET IN A TURN ABOUT 10 MILES SOUTHEAST OF GORGONA ISLAND. A.I. CONTACT WAS REGAINED WITH CONTROL'S HELP AND CLOSING IN, VISUAL WAS OBTAINED AT 1500FT. RANGE.

BANDIT WAS THEN IDENTIFIED AS A JU-88. TARGET WAS TAKING VIOLENT EVASIVE ACTION CONSISTING OF HARD TURNS AND ORBITS.

CLOSING IN, OUR A/C FIRED FOUR SHORT BURSTS TOTALLING ABOUT 1½ SECONDS AND 1 LONG BURST OF TWO SECONDS WITHOUT EFFECT, RANGES VARYING FROM 1000 TO 600FT.

AT THIS TIME CONTACT WAS LOST BUT WAS AGAIN REGAINED IN A HEAD-ON INTERCEPTION, PASSING ON

THE SAME LEVEL ABOUT 50FT. APART. [A DIFFICULT FEAT UNDER THE MOST FAVOURABLE CIRCUM-STANCES]. TURNED ONTO TARGET AND FOLLOWED IT TO THE DECK WHERE IT WAS LOST IN GROUND RETURNS TWO MILES OFF-SHORE FROM LEGHORN HARBOR.

OUR A/C THEN RETURNED TO CONTROL AND RESUMED PATROL.

ANOTHER BOGEY WAS REPORTED AT 0305 SO OUR A/C WAS VECTORED IN A SOUTHEASTERLY DIRECTION AND TURNED OVER TO 'SETSQUARE' CONTROL.

BOGEY WAS IN THE VICINITY OF PIANOSA ISLAND. OUR A/C WAS THEN VECTORED IN A SWEEPING TURN WEST AND NORTH ONTO A PLOT WHICH HAD BECOME A BANDIT.

A.I. CONTACT WAS LOST UNDER 'SETSQUARE' BUT WAS REGAINED UNDER 'BANDBOX' IN THAT AREA. CONTACT OBTAINED, OUR A/C FOLLOWED BANDIT ON THE DECK THRU VERY MILD EVASIVE ACTION AND OBTAINED A VISUAL AT ABOUT 3000FT. RANGE, ALTITUDE 100FT. 20 MILES EAST/NORTHEAST OF CAPRAIA ISLAND.

ALTHOUGH BANDIT'S DORSAL GUNNER OPENED FIRE AT 3000FT. OUR A/C FOLLOWED VIOLENT EVASIVE ACTION AT RANGES VARYING FROM 2000FT TO 6000FT. AT THIS TIME, BANDIT'S DORSAL GUNNER KEPT FIRING NUMEROUS BURSTS AT EXCESS RANGE AND TRACER AIDED IN MAINTAINING CONTACT.

BANDIT WAS VERY EFFICIENT AT KEEPING OUR A/C IN THE MOON-PATH. VISUAL CONTACT WAS FINALLY LOST IN A HARD PORT TURN MADE BY BANDIT.

OUR A/C THEN FOUND BANDIT AGAIN VISUALLY, BANDIT CROSSING FROM PORT TO STARBOARD 90 DEG. TO OUR A/C'S COURSE. OUR A/C THEN FIRED AN EXTREMELY SHORT BURST WITH THREE RINGS DEFLEC-TION FROM 600FT. BUT NO RESULTS WERE OBSERVED. SWINGING STARBOARD, OUR A/C MAINTAINED CONTACT ON BANDIT, HIS DORSAL GUNNER CONTINU-ING FIRE AT SUCH A RANGE THAT HIS TRACER BURNED

OUT BEFORE REACHING OUR A/C.

OUR A/C THEN CLOSED TO APPROX. 1500FT. RANGE IN A PORT TURN AND FIRED A SHORT BURST WITH 1 1/2 RING DEFLECTION BUT STILL NO STRIKES OBSERVED, AND DORSAL GUNNER STILL FIRING. VISUAL CONTACT WAS THEN LOST AGAINST THE DARK MASS OF THE COAST OF ITALY AND A.I. CONTACT WAS LOST IN GROUND RETURNS AND SEA RETURNS OVER THE ENTRANCE TO LEGHORN HARBOR. DURING SECOND CHASE, ALTITUDE WAS FROM 30 TO 500FT.

NO CLAIM WAS MADE.

NARRATIVE OF COMBAT, MORNING OF 19 JULY 1944

OUR A/C WAS CONTROLLED BY 'BANDBOX' CONTROL.

AT 0130, OUR A/C WAS VECTORED ONTO A BANDIT AT SIX MILES RANGE. A/C WAS INSTRUCTED TO INCREASE SPEED AND BROUGHT TO WITHIN 4 MILES OF ENEMY A/C.

A.I. CONTACT WAS ESTABLISHED VERY SHORTLY AFTER AND EVASIVE ACTION BY BANDIT WAS QUITE VIOLENT. OUR A/C THEN CLOSED IN SLOWLY DUE TO EVASIVE ACTION AND LOW ALTITUDE. OUR A/C'S HEIGHT WAS ABOUT 100FT. DURING THE LATTER PART OF THE CHASE WITH AIRSPEED ABOUT 210MPH, BANDIT'S AIRSPEED BEING 200MPH.

OUR A/C WAS CLOSING IN TO 1500FT. RANGE WHEN ITS A.I. EQUIPMENT TEMPORARILY WENT OUT OF COM-MISSION. BEING AT OVERTAKING SPEED, OUR A/C WAS ABLE TO OBTAIN A VISUAL OF THE BANDIT 1000FT. AHEAD, SLIGHTLY ABOVE AND 10 DEGREES TO STARBOARD.

VISIBILITY WAS QUITE HAZY AND IDENTIFICATION WAS VERY DIFFICULT. HOWEVER, THE BANDIT WAS IDENTIFIED AS A JU-88.

OUR A/C FIRED A TWO SECOND BURST FROM 600FT. AND OBSERVED TWO CANNON FLASHES (HIGH EXPLO-SIVES). ONLY ONE CANNON WAS FIRING. VISUAL WAS IMMEDIATELY LOST WHEN BANDIT TURNED TO PORT VERY SHARPLY AND GAVE RETURN FIRE FROM HIS

VENTRAL GUNS. TRACERS PASSED TO OUR A/C'S PORT BUT NO DAMAGE WAS SUSTAINED.

THIS ACTION TOOK PLACE 20 MILES TO 40 MILES NORTH OF CAPE CORSE. OUR A/C IMMEDIATELY ASKED CONTROL FOR HELP AND THEY LOST THE BANDIT TEMPORARILY BUT WERE SOON ABLE TO VECTOR OUR A/C.

OUR A/C'S A.I. EQUIPMENT BEGAN TO WORK AGAIN AND CONTACT WAS AGAIN OBTAINED AT 4 MILES, HOWEVER, BANDIT WAS HEADING NORTH AND SOON FADED FROM OUR A/C'S SCOPE.

CLAIM WAS MADE FOR AND VERIFIED AS ONE JU-88 DAMAGED.

NARRATIVE OF COMBAT, NIGHT OF 20 JULY 1944

OUR A/C, AIRBORNE AT 2140 WAS VECTORED BY 'SETSQUARE' CONTROL STATION ONTO A BOGEY AT 2310.

AT 2315, OUR A/C RECEIVED WORD THAT BOGEY WAS CONFIRMED BANDIT AT 1000FT. ALTITUDE AND AT 2320 OUR A/C MADE CONTACT ON BANDIT JUST SOUTH OF PIANOSA ISLAND.

AT 2325, OUR A/C CALLED THAT HE HAD SHOT DOWN THE ENEMY A/C AND THAT IT HAD HIT THE WATER. OUR A/C AGAIN CALLED AT 2329 TO STATE THAT HE WAS GOING LOWER AND LOOK FOR WRECKAGE.

THIS WAS THE LAST MESSAGE RECEIVED FROM OUR A/C BY THE CONTROLLER.

A SEARCH OF THE AREA AT DAWN REVEALED MUCH DEBRIS FROM BOTH ENEMY AND OWN A/C, INCLUDING DINGHIES FROM BOTH A/C.

IT IS EVIDENT THAT OUR A/C DESTROYED THE ENEMY A/C BEFORE CRASHING HIMSELF. CAUSE OF OWN A/C'S LOSS IS NOT KNOWN.

CLAIM WAS MADE FOR AND VERIFIED AS ONE ENEMY A/C (UNIDENTIFIED) DESTROYED IN THE ABOVE AIRCREW'S NAME. IT IS BELIEVED THAT OUR A/C HIT THE WATER WHEN THE PILOT WENT DOWN TO SEARCH FOR SURVIVORS FOR INTERROGATION.

LOST CREW WAS LT. INGLIS AND F/O HEARNE-RO.

NARRATIVE OF COMBAT, NIGHT OF 19 OCTOBER 1944

OUR A/C WAS AIRBORNE AT 1755 HRS.

AT 1800 HRS, OUR A/C WENT ON PATROL WITH 'MATURE' CONTROL STATION IN THE AREA OF ST. TROPEZ, FRANCE, AT AN ALTITUDE OF 8000FT.

AT 1852 HRS, OUR A/C WAS TURNED OVER TO 'MIMIC' CONTROL STATION, WHO SENT IT DOWN TO DECK LEVEL AND GAVE OUR A/C VECTORS ONTO A BOGEY.

FIRST INFORMATION RECEIVED BY OUR A/C WAS THAT BOGEY WAS FLYING AT DECK LEVEL APPROX. 10 MILES SOUTH OF NICE DOING ORBITS AND CHASE BEGAN AT A RANGE OF 12 MILES.

OUR A/C GAVE CHASE AT 290MPH PLUS AT DECK LEVEL IN GENERAL EASTERLY DIRECTION THROUGH VIOLENT EVASIVE ACTION. TWO FLEETING A.I. CONTACTS WERE OBTAINED AT 4 MILES. BOGEY WAS DOING 300 PLUS MPH AT HEIGHTS RANGING FROM 100 TO 500FT.

AT 1930 HRS, 'MIMIC' STATED THEY COULD HELP OUR A/C NO FURTHER AND IMMEDIATELY AFTERWARDS, A.I. CONTACT WAS OBTAINED AT 3 MILE RANGE, WITH BOGEY READING 40 DEG ABOVE DEAD AHEAD. OWN A/C'S HEIGHT WAS THEN AT 1000FT.

BOTH A/C WERE, AT THE TIME, OVER THE ITALIAN COAST HEADING NORTHEAST. BOGEY BEGAN CLIMBING AND OUR A/C FOLLOWED THRU A.I. CONTACT TO AN ALTITUDE OF 9000FT. WHERE VISUAL WAS OBTAINED AT RANGE OF 500FT. 20 DEG. ABOVE.

OUR A/C CLOSED IN TO 100FT. AND IDENTIFIED BOGEY AS A JU-188, THEN DROPPED BACK TO 400FT. RANGE AND FIRED A LONG BURST FROM DEAD ASTERN 15 DEG. BELOW BANDIT OBSERVING HIGH EXPLOSIVE STRIKES ON REAR FUSELAGE JUST FORWARD OF TAILPLANE. BANDIT FIRED A VERY SHORT BURST OF TRACER WITHOUT RESULT AND FELL OFF TO PORT IN A STEEP SPIRAL DIVE, NEAR VERTICAL IN THE EXCESS OF 4000FT. PER MINUTE RATE OF DESCENT.

VISUAL WAS HELD AND OUR A/C FOLLOWED BANDIT

EARTHWARD FIRING A LONG AND A SHORT BURST ENROUTE. AT 4000FT. ALTITUDE, BANDIT, SHOWING NO INDICATION OF PULLING OUT OF STEEP SPIRAL DIVE, WENT INTO A CLOUD LAYER AND VISUAL WAS LOST AND IMMEDIATELY AFTERWARDS A.I. CONTACT WAS BROKEN.

OUR A/C DID NOT FOLLOW BANDIT THRU CLOUDS AS THE AIRCREW WAS NOT FAMILIAR WITH THE SUR-ROUNDING COUNTRY. POSITION AT THE TIME WAS UNKNOWN BUT APPROXIMATED AS 10-15 MILES SOUTHEAST OF CREMONA, ITALY.

OUR A/C FLEW SOUTHWEST FOR 20 MINUTES, CONTACTED 'MIMIC' AND RESUMED PATROL EAST OF ST. TROPEZ.

ENEMY A/C'S RATE AND MANNER OF DESCENT OVER MOUNTAINOUS TERRAIN JUSTIFIED THIS AIRCREW'S CLAIM OF ONE JU-188 PROBABLY DESTROYED. THIS WAS VERIFIED AS SUCH.

PROBABLY DESTROYED BY LT. H.J. ALLEN AND LT. W.E. GRINNELL.

NARRATIVE OF COMBAT, NIGHT OF 30 NOVEMBER 1944.

OUR AIRCRAFT WAS AIRBORNE AT 2045 HRS ON PATROL MISSION WITH 'TURNSCREW' CONTROL STATION OFF COAST OF NICE.

AT 2213 HRS OUR A/C TURNED OVER TO 'MIMIC' CONTROL STATION AND GIVEN A VECTOR OF 200 DEG. ONTO A BANDIT REPORTED APPROXIMATELY 15 MILES NORTH EAST.

REDUCING ALTITUDE FROM 6000FT. AND MAINTAIN-ING A SPEED OF 280-285MPH OUR A/C OBTAINED A.I. CONTACT AT 2½ MILE RANGE AT HEIGHT OF 1000FT. BANDIT READING 20 DEG. ABOVE DOING APPROXI-MATELY 270MPH. POSITION AT TIME OF CONTACT WAS AT APPROXIMATELY 30 MILES SOUTH, SOUTHEAST OF CANNES, FRANCE.

OUR A/C CLOSED IN TO 2000FT. WHEN VISUAL WAS OBTAINED AT 2250 HRS. ONTO BANDIT WHO WAS FLYING TO OUR STARBOARD GIVING NO EVASIVE

ACTION.

AT RANGE OF 200FT. OUR A/C IDENTIFIED THE BANDIT AS A JU-88. FROM DEAD ASTERN, AT 150FT. RANGE OUR A/C FIRED A SHORT BURST OBSERVING STRIKES ON ENEMY'S STARBOARD WING AND PIECES OF ENEMY WING BREAKING OFF AND STRIKING OUR HORIZONTAL STABILIZER. THE ENEMY A/C THEN PEELED OFF SHARPLY TO PORT

AND WENT INTO A STEEP DIVE LOSING OUR VISUAL AND A.I. CONTACT.

THE ENEMY A/C REPORTED ON 048 DEG. LOSING ALTITUDE AND OUR A/C PURSUED THE ENEMY IN A NORTHEASTERLY COURSE RECEIVING MUCH A.I. INTERFERENCE INDICATING USE OF WINDOW. THE CHASE ENDED IN THE GULF OF GENOVA, ITALY AT 2255 HRS. THE ATTACK APPARENTLY TOOK THE ENEMY BY SURPRISE. THERE WAS NO DAMAGE TO OUR A/C.

NORMAL PATROL WAS RESUMED WITH 'TURNSCREW' WITHOUT FURTHER INCIDENT.

CLAIM WAS MADE FOR AND VERIFIED AS ONE JU-188 DAMAGED BY 2ND LTS ANDERSON AND WELFLEY-RO.

NARRATIVE OF COMBAT, NIGHT OF 15 DECEMBER 1944

OUR AIRCRAFT WAS SCRAMBLED AFTER A BANDIT AT 2240 HRS. AND VECTORED BY 'PINTO' CONTROL STATION. BANDIT REPORTED AT DECK LEVEL SOUTHEAST OF MARSEILLES.

AT 2300 HRS OUR A/C OBTAINED A BRIEF A.I. CONTACT AT 3 ½ MILE RANGE WHILE DOING 270PH. BANDIT WAS HEADING WEST AT HEIGHT OF 200 FT. DOING APPROX. 250MPH. CONTACT WAS LOST WHEN BANDIT TURNED TOWARD US ON PARTIAL HEAD-ON. FAST ENCLOSURE AND INTERFERENCE OF GROUND RETURNS PROHIBITED COMPLETED INTERCEPTION.

WITH HELP OF CONTROL, A.I. CONTACT WAS REGAINED AT 2310 HRS. BANDIT WAS HEADING EAST AT 200FT. SOUTH OF ST. TROPEZ, FRANCE.

OUR A/C CLOSED IN TO 700FT. RANGE WHERE VISUAL WAS OBTAINED AND BANDIT WAS IDENTIFIED AS A JU-188.

OR A/C THEN CLOSED TO 600FT. AND FIRED A TWO SECOND BURST FROM DEAD ASTERN OBSERVING NO RESULTS. VISIBILITY AT TIME RANGED FROM 500FT. PLUS.

VISUAL WAS LOST AS BANDIT STARTED VIOLENT EVASIVE ACTION. CONTINUED CHASE ON A.I. AND AT 2335 ANOTHER VISUAL WAS OBTAINED AND OUR A/C IMMEDIATELY FIRED A ½ SECOND BURST FROM 500FT. RANGE WITH ABOUT 10 DEGREE DEFLECTION AT HEIGHT OF 200FT. OBSERVED STRIKES ON PORT WING OUTBOARD OF ENGINE NACELLE.

LOST VISUAL BUT CONTINUED CHASE AT ALTITUDES VARYING FROM 100 TO 500FT. CONTACT ON A.I. WAS LOST AND REGAINED INTERMITTENTLY DUE TO OUR AIRCRAFT'S BLOWN EXHAUST STACK WHICH GAVE OUR POSITION AWAY WITH 3000FT. RANGE OF ENEMY A/C.

DURING THE CHASE, AFTER TARGET KNEW OF OUR PROXIMITY, THE EVASIVE ACTION VARIED ACCORDING TO WHETHER THE ENEMY COULD SEE OUR A/C APPROACHING OR NOT.

AT 0005 HRS. CONTACT WAS LOST IN GROUND RETURNS IN VICINITY OF SPEZIA, ITALY. VECTORED HOME BY 'TURNSCREW', 'MIMIC', 'GALLEY' AND 'DOGLEG' CONTROLS AND HOMER.

CLAIM WAS MADE FOR AND VERIFIED AS ON JU-188 DAMAGED BY MAJ C.R. MCCRAY AND 1ST LT R. D. HAMILTON-RO.

NARRATIVE OF COMBAT, MORNING OF 17 FEBRUARY 1945

OUR AIRCRAFT WAS AIRBORNE AT 2325 FOR PATROL MISSION WITH 'TURNSCREW' CONTROL STATION.

WAS VECTORED AFTER BANDIT REPORTED 20 MILES EAST OF CAP MELE, FRANCE HEADING SOUTHWEST AT HEIGHT OF 1000FT. DOING 230MPH. FIFTY MILES SOUTHEAST OF NICE.

BANDIT TURNED IN EASTERLY DIRECTION AND OUR A/C OBTAINED A.I. CONTACT AT 0225 HRS.

AT 5 MILE RANGE. WHILE OUR A/C WAS AT HEIGHT OF

2500 FT. SPEED WAS INCREASED TO 300MPH IN DIVE TO HEIGHT OF 1000FT. CLOSING IN RAPIDLY.

WHEN RANGE CLOSED TO 8000FT. BANDIT COMMENCED A SLOW CLIMB. AT 1500FT. RANGE OUR A/C SIGHTED GREEN TAIL LIGHT 10 DEG. ABOVE AND CLIMBED TO FOLLOW INTO INTERCEPTION. BANDIT MADE HEIGHT OF 1800FT. WITH OUR A/C DIRECTLY BEHIND WITH CONSIDERABLE OVERTAKING SPEED.

WHILE OUR A/C DIRECTLY BEHIND BANDIT AND APPROX. 10 DEG. BELOW BANDIT'S DORSAL GUNS OPENED FIRE UPON US WITH NO RESULT. HAVING EXCESS SPEED OUR A/C BROKE OFF TO PORT AND OBTAINED A CLEAR PROFILE VIEW OF BANDIT AND IDENTIFIED SAME AS AN ME 210/410.

WHEN OFF TO PORT OF ENEMY A/C, OUR A/C THROTTLED BACK TOO ABRUPTLY CAUSING AN EXHAUST FLAME AND ENEMY A/C AGAIN FIRED UPON OUR A/C AND AGAIN WITHOUT RESULT.

OUR A/C THEN LOST ENOUGH SPEED TO SLIDE IN BEHIND AT WHICH TIME TARGET COMMENCED TO DIVE. FROM A RANGE OF 400FT. OUR A/C FIRED A SIX SECOND BURST, RESULTS NOT OBSERVED AND RECEIVING AGAIN INEFFECTIVE RETURN FIRE.

WHILE STILL IN A SLIGHT DIVE OUR A/C AGAIN FIRED A BURST OF ABOUT 2½ SECOND DURATION AND OBSERVED ENEMY'S PORT ENGINE EXPLODE WITH A FLAME WHICH MOMENTARILY ILLUMINATED THE ENTIRE PORT SIDE OF THE ENEMY AIRCRAFT.

THE ENEMY'S PORT WING APPEARED TO BREAK OFF JUST OUTBOARD OF THE ENGINE NACELLE. THE ENEMY CEASED FIRING UPON OUR A/C AND APPEARED TO BE LOSING HEIGHT AND FORWARD SPEED.

AT A HEIGHT OF 1200FT. OUR A/C PASSED OVER WHERE THE ENEMY HAD BEEN, PULLING UP TO AVOID LARGE FRAGMENTS OF BURNING OR GLOWING DEBRIS.

AT 1500FT. OUR A/C FLEW STRAIGHT AND LEVEL FOR A FEW MINUTES AND CONTACTED 'TURNSCREW'. PLOT OF BANDIT HAD FADED FROM THEM AND WE WERE VECTORED HOME.

THE ENEMY A/C WHEN LAST SEEN WAS IN A 20-30 DEG. VERTICAL DIVE AND 25-35 DEG. STARBOARD BANK AT 1000FT. ALTITUDE. THE ENEMY A/C WAS NOT ACTUALLY SEEN TO CRASH. THE DAMAGE INFLICTED WAS OF SUCH VITAL NATURE THAT THE ENEMY SEEMED IMPOS-SIBLE OF SUSTAINED FLIGHT OR OF CRASH LANDING.

CLAIM WAS MADE FOR AND NOT VERIFIED AS ON ME 210/410 PROBABLY DESTROYED BY 2ND LTS R. W. CONDON AND R.M. CORNWALL-RO.

APPENDIX VI

Fighter Director Terms

The following are common terms used between GCI controllers and aircrews, taken from Combined Communication Board Publication 0123:

W/T (MORSE CODE)	R/T (VOICE)	MEANING
AM-MN	Ammo Minus	Have less than half ammunition left
AM-PS	Ammo Plus	Have more than half ammunition left
AM-0	Ammo Zero	Have no ammunition left
AK	Anchored	Am orbiting a visible orbit point
AG	Angels	Height in thousands of feet
BT	Bandit	Identified enemy aircraft
BG	Bogey	Unidentified aircraft
BS	Bombers	High-level bombers
BU	Buster	Fly at normal full speed
CN	Chickens	Friendly fighters
CA	Clara	Radar screen is clear of any contacts
CL	Close	Keep near directing station (could be a ship as well)
--	Make your cockerel crow	Switch on your IFF (the electronic box that sent out electronic signal to identify friendly aircraft)
--	Strangle cockerel	Switch off your IFF. Later

		'cockerel' was replaced with 'canary'
--	Flash your weapon	Turn on your airborne intercept radar (AI)
--	Weapon bent	My AI is unserviceable
--	Contact	I have an indication on my AI
--	Contact lost	I have lost contact
--	Punch	You should be obtaining a contact on your AI.
--	Judy	I am taking over control of this interception
FS	Fishes	Torpedo aircraft
FD	Freddie	Fighter directing ship (GCI afloat)
FY	Friendly	Aircraft identified as friendly
FL	Fuel	Quantity of fuel remaining, e.g. 'Fuel 42' means 42 gallons remaining
GA	Gate	Fly at maximum possible speed; not to be maintained for more than five minutes
GR	Grand slam	Enemy aircraft shot down
HS	Hawks	Dive bombers
HU	Heads up	Enemy aircraft got through, i.e. unsuccessful interception
RC	Hey Rube	Rendezvous over directing ship. Also, call made when taking up assigned patrol area
LF	Left (Port)	Alter course to left (normally means 30 degree turn)
LT	Lights	Identify yourself now by turning on navigation lights
MT	Mattress	Below cloud
Q	O'clock	Aircraft in clock code sector e.g. 'Chickens at 1 o'clock'
OR	Orbit	Circle and search
PK	Pancake	Land, refuel, rearm. Can be directive or informative

PY	Popeye	In cloud
QL	Quilt	Above cloud
RS	Rats	Identified enemy fighter
RH	Request homing	Request course to steer for home base
RT	Right (starboard)	Normally a 30 degree right turn
SA	Saunter	Fly at lowest possible cruising speed
SC	Scramble	Take off, set course and climb, e.g. 'Scramble zero zero one zero, angels ten'
TL	Tally ho	Enemy aircraft sighted
VC	Vector	Alter course to new heading e.g. "Vector zero six zero".

APPENDIX VII

417th Squadron Distinguished Unit Citation

Under the provisions of Circular 335, War Department, 1943, and Circular 73, MTOUSA, 12 May 1945, the 417th Night Fighter Squadron is cited for outstanding performance of duty in action against the enemy in the Mediterranean Theater of Operations, on the night of 28 December 1944.

After rendering unceasing protection by night to ships and personnel being assembled in Mediterranean waters for the invasion of southern France and fighting off early enemy attempts to bomb troops and supplies at secured beachheads, the 417th Night Fighter Squadron was given the heavy responsibility of protecting the entire coast of southern France and particularly the port of Marseilles, one of the two existing arteries through which all vital supplies and reinforcements were fed to the fighting fronts in western Europe. In spite of extremely adverse flying conditions, including freezing temperatures, persistently low ceiling and 70-mile-an-hour winds common to the Rhône Valley, weather which grounded almost all other aircraft in France, air crews of the 417th Night Fighter Squadron, in complete defiance of the hazards involved, resolutely performed their assigned task and turned away enemy attempts to prepare Marseilles for bombing by reconnaissance and path-finding. On 12 December 1944, the squadron was informed the enemy would attempt to transport a large number of high government officials, Nazi leaders and gold bullion to a neutral country for the purpose of intensifying their war effort against the Allies and that every effort must be made to thwart such an attempt. With a strength of ten ancient Beaufighters, many of which had been salvaged, rebuilt and returned to service, the 417th Night Fighter Squadron accepted the tremendous strain placed on both men and machines. Despite ceaseless gales and bitter cold in which ground crews worked without shelter of hangars or tents, and burdened with the mental hazard of a depressingly long list of casualties suffered from weather, watered fuel, and mechanical failures of the out-moded Beaufighters, air crews courageously went aloft on each night. Gallantly and with complete disregard for discomforts, dangers and discouraging weather conditions both ground and air personnel determinedly carried out their dual mission. On the night of 28 December 1944, culminating weeks of persevering effort, a 417th Beaufighter made contact with and identified a four-engined German transport. Courageously and skillfully maneuvering at less than 20 feet above water, the determined crew, after an unrelenting pursuit through the darkness, opened fire with accurate bursts which sent the enemy aircraft crashing into flames into the sea. Displaying the highest sense of duty in carrying out their assigned missions despite inescapable and disheartening risks, the 417th Night Fighter Squadron, paying heavily in gallant crewmen and aircraft, accomplished this vital interdiction and at the same time maintained continuous and effective patrol of the Marseilles port area. The courage, devotion and technical skill displayed by the personnel of this squadron in the face of extraordinary hazards reflect the highest credit upon themselves and the Military Service of the United States.

BY COMMAND OF BRIGADIER GENERAL MYERS

APPENDIX VIII

USAAF NIGHT-FIGHTER SQUADRONS OF WORLD WAR II

Unit	Date Activated	Aircraft	Air Force area of operations
6TH NFS	9/1/43	P-70, P-38, P-61	7th AF/Central, S/SW Pacific
414th NFS	26/1/43	Beaufighter, P-61	12th AF/ MTO, ETO
415th NFS	10/2//43	Beaufighter, P-61	12th AF/MTO, ETO
416th NFS	20/2/43	Beaufighter, Mosquito, P-61	12th AF/MTO, ETO
417th NFS	20/2/43	Beaufighter, P-61	12th AF/MTO, ETO
418th NFS	1/4/43	P-70, P-38, P-61	5th AF/SW, W Pacific
419th NFS	1/4/43	P-70, P-38, P-61	13th AF/S SW Pacific
420th NFS	1/6/43	P-70, P-61	4th AF/Stateside training unit
421st NFS	1/5/43	P-70, P-38, P-61	5th AF/SW, W Pacific
422d NFS	1/8/43	P-61	9th AF/ETO
423d NFS	1/9/43	P-70, A-20	9th AF/Redesignated 155 Night Photo Reconnaissance Squadron, 22/6/44
424th NFS	24/11/43	P-70	4th AF/Stateside training unit
425th NFS	1/12/43	P-61	9th AF/ETO
426th NFS	1/1/44	P-61	10th & 14th AF/CBI
427th NFS	1/2/44	P-61	10th AF/CBI
547th NFS	1/3/44	P-70, P-38, P-61	5th AF/SW, W Pacific
548th NFS	10/4/44	P-61	7th AF/W Pacific
549th NFS	1/5/44	P-61	7th AF/W Pacific
550th NFS	1/6/44	P-61	13th AF/SW Pacific

BIBLIOGRAPHY

Books and Journals

Michael Allen: *Pursuit Through Darkened Skies: An Ace Night Fighter Crew in World War II*, Crowood Press, 2004

Victor Bingham: *Bristol Beaufighter*, Airlife Publishing Ltd., 1994

Chaz Bowyer: *Beaufighter at War*, Ian Allen Ltd., London, 1976

Braxton R. Eisel: 'Signal Aircraft Warning Battalions in the Southwest Pacific in World War II', *Air Power History*, Vol. 51, No. 3, Fall 2004

Braxton R. Eisel: 'Twenty Years of Service: The Bristol Beaufighter', *Wings* Magazine, Vol. 34, No. 6, June 2004

Colin Latham and Anne Stobbs: *Radar: A Wartime Miracle*, Sutton Publishing Ltd., 1997

Stephen L. McFarland: *Conquering the Night Skies: Army Air Forces Night Fighters at War*, Air Forces History and Museums Programs, 1997

Maurer Maurer: *Air Force Combat Units of World War II*, Franklin Witts, 1992

Official History of the 417th Night Fighter Squadron, US Army Air Forces

Official History of the 415th Night Fighter Squadron, US Army Air Forces

Official History of the 414th Night Fighter Squadron, US Army Air Forces

Gary R. Pape and Ronald C. Harrison: *Queen of the Midnight Skies: The Story of America's Air Force Night Fighters*, Schiffer Publishing Ltd., West Chester, PA., 1992

Paul Peyron: *C'est La Guerre: A Personal Memoir of the 417th Night Fighter Squadron of the Second World War*, Professional Help Press, Baker City, OR, 1994

C.F. Rawnsley and Robert Wright: *Night Fighter*, Crecy Publishing Ltd., 1998 (first published 1957 by Collins Publishing)

Wolfgang W. E. Samuel: *American Raiders: The Race to Capture the Luftwaffe's Secrets*, University Press of Mississippi, 2004

Frederick O. Sargent, Sargent: *An Unofficial History of the 415th Night Fighter Squadron*, Madison, WI., 1946

Jerry Scutts: *Beaufighters in Action*, Squadron/Signal Publication
   No. 153, Carrolton, TX, 1995
P.W. Stahl: *KG 200: The True Story*, Jane's, 1981.
Warren E. Thompson: 'More Than Equal', *FlyPast Magazine*,
   January 2003
Daniel D. Whitney, ed: *417th Night Fighter Squadron: An
   Illustrated History of One of the First USAAF Nightfighting
   Squadrons Serving in England, North Africa, Corsica, France,
   Germany*, 2001.

Archives

National Museum of the United States Air Force Archives,
Wright-Patterson Air Force Base, Dayton, Ohio.

Websites

www.nasm.si.edu/research/aero/aircraft/norhtrop_p61.htm

www.maam.org/p61/p61spec.html

www.acepilots.com/planes/p61_black_widow.html

www.bankofcanada.ca/en/gold/gold97-3.htm

www.cia.gov/studies/summer00/art04.html

Personal Papers/Letters

Robert Condon
Robert McCullen
William Rial

Correspondence/Interviews

George Aubill, Major (ret), USAF
Terence Carter
Dr Morris Dalton
Joe Draper
Richard Fryklund
Thomas Hart
Earl Hisset
Rayford Jeffrey, Major (ret), USAF
Dr Arthur Katzburg, Col (ret), USAF
Thomas E. Luke
Carroll Poole
John Roberson
William Vincent, Maj Gen (ret), Canadian Forces
James Van Voorhis
Richard Ziebart

Index

Numbered Military Units